SHOCK AND *Awe*

Tasting God's outrageous grace

Published by
The Bible Reading Fellowship
15 The Chambers, Vineyard
Abingdon OX14 3FE
United Kingdom
Tel: +44 (0)1865 319700
Email: enquiries@brf.org.uk
Website: www.brf.org.uk

ISBN 978 1 84101 641 2

First published 2009
10 9 8 7 6 5 4 3 2 1 0

Acknowledgments
Unless otherwise stated, scripture quotations are taken from the Holy Bible, New International Version, copyright © 1973, 1978, 1984 by International Bible Society, are used by permission of Hodder & Stoughton Publishers, a division of Hodder Headline Ltd. All rights reserved. 'NIV' is a registered trademark of International Bible Society. UK trademark number 1448790.

Scripture quotations from *The Message*. Copyright © by Eugene H. Peterson 1993, 1994, 1995. Used by permission of NavPress Publishing Group.

'Not by might' by Rob Lacey. Used by kind permission of Sandra Lacey.

Collect for Christmas Day and Collect for New Year's Eve from *Celebrating Common Prayer*, reproduced by kind permission of Continuum International Publishing Group.

'A marvellous healing' by Gerard Kelly, from *Spoken Worship*, Grand Rapids: Zondervan, 2007. Used by permission.

Extract from 'The Chapel' by R.S. Thomas, from *Collected Poems 1945–1990*, published by J.M. Dent, a division of The Orion Publishing Group, London. Copyright © R.S. Thomas 1993.

A catalogue record for this book is available from the British Library

Printed in Singapore by Craft Print International Ltd

Tasting God's outrageous grace

IAN COFFEY

For Mike and Rosemary,
with gratitude for
friends who truly care

Acknowledgments

When first approached to write this book, I was fairly convinced I would have to say no, but, in the time I was mulling over the decision, my life took a quite dramatic and unexpected turn.

As things developed, I was able to find a generous slice of time between moving back from France (where we had been serving an international congregation just outside Geneva) and starting a new job at Moorlands College on the south coast of England.

Once I adapted to writing about Advent during the height of an English summer (a task made slightly easier by some days when the weather looked much like December!), I settled quickly and found much fulfilment in preparing these daily studies. I am grateful to God for the opportunity to reflect and write on some wonderful passages from scripture and to discover again in new ways that 'the unfolding of your words gives light' (Psalm 119:130). I trust that you will enjoy reading the studies as much as I enjoyed writing them.

This book is dedicated to two close and long-standing friends, Mike and Rosemary Rimmington, who, on learning of our decision to move back to the UK, immediately opened their spacious home to us for almost four months. More than that, they went out of their way to share friendship and love with us at a time when it was much needed. Their home, in the heart of rural England, was where this book was written in the most tranquil surroundings any writer could wish for. Thanks are due to them for providing a shelter from the storm and a place of healing and renewal.

The team at BRF are delightful people to work with and, as this is my fourth book with them, I speak from experience. Thanks to the whole team and, in particular, Naomi Starkey who has kept me (largely) on track.

As usual, my wife Ruth has provided all the support, constructive criticism and encouragement that were needed. I am always in her debt and enjoy our shared journey more than ever.

Contents

Introduction

Advent is a season of surprise.

The Bible readings and meditations in this book will regularly remind us that the incarnation of Jesus Christ, God's Son, was met with incredulity, wonder and astonishment. The hymn writer of a previous generation, Charles Wesley (1707–88), expressed it so well:

Let earth and heaven combine,
angels and men agree,
to praise in songs divine
the incarnate Deity,
our God contracted to a span,
incomprehensibly made man.

When I began to think about these Advent readings and how we might rediscover the wonder of the incarnation, I was gripped by a phrase that wouldn't let go of me: 'shock and awe'.

Mention the words 'shock and awe' to many people and they are instantly connected with the contentious military campaign launched against Iraq in 2003. But the phrase itself was borrowed by military commanders from a strategy developed some years previously at the National Defense University of the United States of America.

Two military strategists observed a lesson from history, stretching back many centuries: put simply, if you can overwhelm your enemy with an early strike of decisive force, then their will to resist is broken. By the process of shock, your opponent is awed into submission.[1]

Leaving aside the controversy surrounding the decision to invade Iraq (a valid and important discussion for another place), I was struck by the description 'shock and awe' and the tacit assumption that this could only be achieved by bombs, bullets, might and power.

The kingdom of God is about shock and awe, but of a wholly

different kind. The gospel of the Lord Jesus Christ is of a king who stoops to conquer, who washes the feet of his followers, takes the place of a lowly slave and is willing to pay the ultimate price of redeeming love through an ignominious and unjust death. There is no apparent might or power in a baby in a manger, or a man riding on a donkey surrounded by cheering children, or one nailed to a cross before a jeering crowd. But the important word here is 'apparent'.

The shock of the incarnation of the servant-king has led to a different kind of awe—not that of the subjugated, terrorised and submissive, but rather the awe of wonder, incredulity and love. Isaac Watts (1674–1748) had it right when he wrote that nothing in the whole of creation could respond to such amazing love without the giving of its whole self to God in grateful submission and service.[2]

This is the breathless awe of love.

Rob Lacey expresses the upside-down values of the kingdom of God (which are in direct contrast to a widely accepted view of power) in his poem, 'Not by might'.[3] (Like many poems, its best value will be discovered by reading it aloud.)

Not by right (nor by write), nor by repute,
Not by clout, nor by cute,
Not by colour, nor by drive,
Not by thorough, nor by dive,
Not by charm, nor by choice,
Not by virile, nor by voice,
Not by looks, nor by loud,
Not by luck, nor by endowed,
Not by favours, nor by fight,
Not by brave, nor by bright,
Not by polish, nor by gleam,
Not by rule, nor by regime,
Not by focus, nor by tact,
Not by passion, nor by pact,
Not by push, nor by press,

Not by name, nor by address,
Not by steal, nor by sword,
Not by appeal, nor by applaud,
Not by might, nor by power,
But by my Spirit,
Says the Lord.

The big story of the Bible speaks of God's great rescue project for lost people. The theme of the story is grace (undeserved love) and his method, shock and awe. This is a God of surprises who chooses unlikely people and works in unusual ways. Our studies through this season of Advent will help us dip into that story and see first-hand what it involves.

We begin with Abram in the first book of the Bible, Genesis, and we conclude with a vision of God's future plan in the final book of Revelation. In between, we shall consider what it means to be people of faith, trusting God's promises and encountering him in new ways in our daily lives. We shall consider some of the gifts that grace brings and think about what it means practically to live as followers of Christ and as people of hope. It's my hope that this will be a positive learning experience as the Spirit of God impresses and underlines truth for us. I am reminded of Mohandas Gandhi's advice: 'Live as if you were to die tomorrow. Learn as if you were to live for ever.'

The studies have been prepared on the basis of daily readings over the six weeks of Advent, but a study guide has been included for those who may wish to compare notes with a wider group.

My prayer is that these studies will give us a deeper glimpse of what it means to taste outrageous grace and to live in the good of it. In writing, I have been encouraged by some words of Archbishop Rowan Williams:

A human being is holy not because he or she triumphs by willpower over chaos and guilt and leads a flawless life, but because that life shows the victory of God's faithfulness in the midst of disorder and imperfection.

The church is holy... not because it is the gathering of the good and the well behaved, but because it speaks of the triumph of grace in the coming together of strangers and sinners, who, miraculously trust one another enough to join in common repentance and common praise... Humanly speaking, holiness is always like this: God's endurance in the middle of our refusal of him, his capacity to meet every refusal with the gift of himself.[4]

Let's explore this outrageous grace.

1–7 DECEMBER

Legacy

If you are a Christian, the story that tells you who you are is not the story of your parents, ancestors, ethnic group or social class. It is, instead, the story of the Bible—the promise to Abraham, deliverance from slavery to Egypt and sin, and the gift of land to landless Israelites and life to dead sinners. This story of promise, deliverance and gift is your family history, the story that defines you.[5]

GRAHAM TOMLIN

We begin our Advent studies by looking at the topic of faith and considering some of its different aspects.

✣

— 1 DECEMBER —

Faith that walks

The Lord had said to Abram, 'Leave your country, your people and your father's household and go to the land I will show you. I will make you into a great nation and I will bless you; I will make your name great, and you will be a blessing. I will bless those who bless you, and whoever curses you I will curse; and all peoples on earth will be blessed through you.' So Abram left, as the Lord had told him; and Lot went with him. Abram was seventy-five years old when he set out from Haran. He took his wife Sarai, his nephew Lot, all the possessions they had accumulated and the people they had acquired in Haran, and they set out for the land of Canaan, and they arrived there.

GENESIS 12:1–5

My wife and I lived abroad for several years. I remember the work involved in moving—finding the best removal company, organising a house to rent, opening bank accounts, locating doctors and dentists, insuring the car—and all in a foreign language. We are glad we did it as the experience brought many good things—not least the capacity to empathise with anyone who announces, 'I am moving to work abroad.'

Abram faced a much bigger challenge. God asked him to set out for an unknown destination.

His family had lived in the city of Ur (11:31), located in the region we know as southern Iraq. God had begun to speak to Abram and told him to leave everything familiar and secure and set out for somewhere better, yet to be revealed.

Abram and his family settled for a time in a place called Haran, a bustling caravan city. The Bible doesn't tell us why he took the decision to stay there: it may have been due to circumstances beyond his control. During this time, his father Terah died and Abram and his entourage then journeyed on towards the land of Canaan. This sets the scene for the remarkable promise that God gave to Abram—a promise that has implications for us as well.

It is not clear from Genesis when the promise was made—it could date back to the time when he was living in Ur—but the details are very clear. The promise is made up of seven strands set out in our reading.

- From Abram will come a great nation.
- Abram will be blessed by God.
- Abram's name will be made great.
- He will be a blessing.
- Those who bless him (treat him well) will be blessed by God.
- Those who curse him (treat him badly) will be cursed by God.
- All peoples on earth will be blessed through Abram.

I can't begin to imagine the impact this news must have had on Abram. My mind is filled with questions. How did he know that this was God speaking and not his overactive imagination? Did he tell his wife and family about the promise? Did he have doubts on the journey? What did his friends in Ur and Haran say about the move?

The Bible doesn't answer my questions but leaves me with this faith-filled phrase: 'So Abram left, as the Lord had told him' (v. 4). That's all I need to know. Abram's faith led to obedient action, and that meant taking a long walk to a new place that God would show him at some future date.

We sometimes make the mistake of thinking that everything needs to be mapped out and planned before we take the step of faith. If that were so, then faith would not be necessary as the path ahead would be obvious. Faith means trusting God when sometimes all we can see is the next step. As we take that step, we trust that the next one will become visible.

Is there a step of faith and obedience that you need to take? Let Abram's example inspire you.

— Reflect —

We live by faith, not by sight.

2 CORINTHIANS 5:7

Father God, teach me to walk by faith, trusting completely in your fatherly care. Amen

✣

— 2 DECEMBER —

Faith that believes

After this, the word of the Lord came to Abram in a vision: 'Do not be afraid, Abram. I am your shield, your very great reward.' But Abram said, 'O Sovereign Lord, what can you give me since I remain childless and the one who will inherit my estate is Eliezer of Damascus?' And Abram said, 'You have given me no children; so a servant in my household will be my heir.' Then the word of the Lord came to him: 'This man will not be your heir, but a son coming from your own body will be your heir.' He took him outside and said, 'Look up at the heavens and count the stars—if indeed you can count them.' Then he said to him, 'So shall your offspring be.' Abram believed the Lord, and he credited it to him as righteousness.

GENESIS 15:1–6

The former British Cabinet Minister, Jonathan Aitken, has written and spoken openly of his own journey to faith and transformation through Jesus Christ.[6] He describes what he calls his 'Sunday Christian' phase, saying that in those days he belonged to a wing of Anglicanism known as the 'Church Reluctant'! He makes an important point that it's possible to attend church and go through the rituals of faith without their having a direct influence on the rest of our lives.

Abram, however, was someone whose faith caused him to reshape his life. Today's reading begins with the words 'After this…' because the story has taken an unexpected turn. Abram's nephew, Lot, was caught up in a battle between neighbouring warlords and was captured. The news reached Abram, who mustered over 300 of his men who were trained fighters. In a surprise night raid, they secured the release of Lot and his family (see Genesis 14:12–16). The Bible details the circumstances in such a way that we understand this remarkable victory as an act of God on Abram's behalf (vv. 18–19).

Hot on the heels of this victory came a night-time conversation with God, which brought a renewed promise. Abram and his wife Sarai were childless. It was the custom in parts of the Middle East that a childless man could adopt a male servant to become the heir of his estate. This may seem strange to our Western minds but, in a culture where the extended family would include trusted servants, it was one way to preserve a family name and line.

When the Lord told Abram, 'I am your shield, your very great reward' (v. 1), Abram's response was one of utter honesty. How could God bless him when his servant Eliezer was to become his nominated heir rather than a natural-born son? Abram was acting in a way that some call 'honest to God', which is a good example to follow. Rather than wrapping up our feelings in religious clichés, it is better to express what is really happening inside.

His honest response led to an astonishing revelation. God took him outside to look up into the night sky and gaze at thousands of pinpricks of light. 'Count the stars,' the Lord said. 'Go on, try and count them, if you can. Because that is how many people will come from a son born from your own body' (see v. 5).

Then follows a simple sentence that reverberates with theological significance: 'Abram believed the Lord, and he credited it to him as righteousness' (v. 6). God, in his grace, accounted Abram as righteous on the basis of his willingness to believe and take God at his word. Elsewhere the Bible describes this as 'the righteousness that comes by faith' (Hebrews 11:7).

Abram's faith went beyond simply believing in God. He believed God.

What are you believing God for today? Is there a promise that you need to recall and bring before God in your prayers?

— Reflect —

'From that one man [Abram] will come in time a family, a tribe and a nation. Abram was that person, the Christopher Columbus of faith, who set off not knowing where, leaving all that was familiar and comfortable, because God had called him to do so.'

COLIN SINCLAIR[7]

✣

— 3 DECEMBER —

Faith that laughs

Now the Lord was gracious to Sarah as he had said, and the Lord did for Sarah what he had promised. Sarah became pregnant and bore a son to Abraham in his old age, at the very time God had promised him. Abraham gave the name Isaac to the son Sarah bore him. When his son Isaac was eight days old, Abraham circumcised him, as God commanded him. Abraham was a hundred years old when his son Isaac was born to him. Sarah said, 'God has brought me laughter, and everyone who hears about this will laugh with me.' And she added, 'Who would have said to Abraham that Sarah would nurse children? Yet I have borne him a son in his old age.'

GENESIS 21:1–7

Naming a child is special. Often, behind the name that is chosen lies much careful thought. The name may honour a loved parent or friend or be wrapped in reasons that are special.

Abraham[8] gave his son the name Isaac, which means 'he laughs', and Isaac's mother, Sarah, explains the reason for such a happy choice. God brought laughter to this family through the miracle-gift of this baby boy. Abraham was 100 years old when the wonderful event occurred and Sarah herself was well past the age of childbearing. This was a miracle that set the neighbours talking, and the news probably spread like a bush fire.

Not only was Isaac's birth a cause for laughter, but the confirmation of God's promise a year previously had had the same effect on an eavesdropping Sarah (see Genesis 18:9–15). The news had made Abraham chuckle earlier, too (see 17:17). Joy embraced this family, which had waited a long time for God to keep his word.

The Bible has much to say about the gift of joy, not least that it is part of the fruit of the Holy Spirit (see Galatians 5:22). Joy means more than feeling happy; it is the strengthening presence of God that touches the deepest part of our being. One hymn writer described it as 'joy that seekest me through pain',[9] recognizing its capacity to transcend the greatest grief.

C.S. Lewis maintained that 'Joy is the serious business of heaven',[10] and the psalmist declared, 'You will fill me with joy in your presence, with eternal pleasures at your right hand' (Psalm 16:11), while Paul urged his Christian friends to 'Rejoice in the Lord always. I will say it again: rejoice!' (Philippians 4:4).

Joy and rejoicing, it seems, are an important aspect of our faith. So why does joy sometimes seem so hard to find?

The writer and pastor John Ortberg tells a delightful story of bath time with his young daughter, Mallory. She had a special song that she sang at happy times, known as 'Dee dah day', often accompanied by an enthusiastic dance. On this occasion, Ortberg was in a hurry and the little girl's insistence on her song and dance routine met with a grumpy 'Hurry up!' from her dad, who wanted to dry and dress her before getting back to important things. She stopped him in his tracks with a question: 'Why?' He saw not a defiant toddler refusing to cooperate, but a child for whom celebration was part of life—challenging the grown-up view of a world of timetables, mortgages, deadlines and pressures. He writes:

Life is not that way for Mallory. Her self is unstuffed. She just lives. Life is a series of 'dee dah day' moments. Not every moment of life is happy, of course. There are still occasions that call for tears—skinned knees, lost friends. But each moment is pregnant with possibility. Mallory doesn't miss many of them. She is teaching me about joy. And I need to learn. Joy is at the heart of God's plan for human beings. Jesus came as the Joy-bringer. The joy we see in the happiest child is but a fraction of the joy that resides in the heart of God.[11]

— Reflect —

The joy of the Lord is your strength.

NEHEMIAH 8:10

Father, grant me today your gift of joy that brings your strength. Amen

✣

— 4 DECEMBER —

Faith that gives

The angel of the Lord called to Abraham from heaven a second time and said, 'I swear by myself, declares the Lord, that because you have done this and have not withheld your son, your only son, I will surely bless you and make your descendants as numerous as the stars in the sky and as the sand on the seashore. Your descendants will take possession of the cities of their enemies, and through your offspring all nations on earth will be blessed, because you have obeyed me.' Then Abraham returned to his servants, and they set off together for Beersheba. And Abraham stayed in Beersheba.

GENESIS 22:15–19

This chapter of scripture is not easy to understand but, as we dig, we will uncover rich seams of truth.

It seems incomprehensible that God would ask Abraham to sacrifice his son and even harder to understand that a loving father would be willing to consider it. Are these the actions of a God of love, and of a man of faith?

The beginning of the chapter tells us, 'Some time later, God tested Abraham' (v. 1), and the incident should be read in this light. God was testing the depth and quality of Abraham's faith, and on this occasion he passed with flying colours. There had been other times in his walk of faith when Abraham hadn't done so well, so this event marks progress in his journey with God.[12]

In the New Testament, Abraham's obedience is held up as a shining example: 'Abraham reasoned that God could raise the dead, and figuratively speaking, he did receive Isaac back from death' (Hebrews 11:19). Abraham believed that God knew what he was doing. If God could bring about Isaac's birth through a miracle, then God had power to raise him from the dead as well. That is astonishing faith!

Our reading tells how God praised Abraham's obedience and reaffirmed the covenant to bless him and make him a blessing to others.

There is a deeper significance to this incident, though, which has to do with the place where it happened. We read that it was in the region of Moriah, which, in today's geography, is the centre of Jerusalem. It became the site of Solomon's famous temple, and today is occupied by the Dome of the Rock, an impressive Muslim mosque built in AD691. Inside is a large outcrop of rock, identified as the traditional site for the intended sacrifice of Isaac, which remains special in the Jewish, Christian and Islamic faiths alike.

Jerusalem was the city where, centuries later, Jesus Christ, God's Son, was crucified as the atoning sacrifice for our sins. Some see in Abraham's willingness to sacrifice Isaac a foreshadowing or preview of what would take place when Jesus died at Golgotha in that same region of Moriah. The respected Bible teacher David Pawson has written:

God stopped Abraham at a crucial point and provided another sacrifice, a ram with its head caught in thorns. Centuries later, John the Baptist would say of Jesus, 'Behold the "ram" of God that takes away the sins of the world'. The word 'lamb' is often applied to Jesus, but little cuddly lambs were never offered for sacrifice—the sacrifices were one-year-old rams with horns. Jesus is depicted in the Book of Revelation as the ram with seven horns signifying strength—'a ram of God'. God provided a ram for Abraham to offer in place of his son, a ram with his head caught in the thorns, and God also announced a new name to himself: 'I am always your provider'. At that same spot another young man in his early thirties was sacrificed with his head in thorns. Do you see there a picture of Jesus?[13]

In the story of Abraham, who was willing to sacrifice his precious son, we have a foreshadowing of a greater Father 'who did not spare his own Son, but gave him up for us all' (Romans 8:32).

What does Abraham teach us about faith that gives?

— Reflect —

'Love in action is a harsh and dreadful thing compared with love in dreams.'

FATHER ZOSSIMA IN FYODOR DOSTOEVSKY'S *THE BROTHERS KARAMAZOV* (1880)

✣

— 5 DECEMBER —

Faith that endures

Against all hope, Abraham in hope believed and so became the father of many nations, just as it had been said to him, 'So shall your offspring be.' Without weakening in his faith, he faced the fact that his body was as good as dead—since he was about a hundred years old—and that Sarah's womb was also dead. Yet he did not waver through unbelief regarding the promise of God, but was strengthened in his faith and gave glory to God, being fully persuaded that God had power to do what he had promised. This is why 'it was credited to him as righteousness'. The words 'it was credited to him' were written not for him alone, but also for us, to whom God will credit righteousness—for us who believe in him who raised Jesus our Lord from the dead. He was delivered over to death for our sins and was raised to life for our justification.

ROMANS 4:18–25

A boy in Sunday school was asked to give a definition of faith. 'Believing things you know aren't true' was his response—and I guess he is not alone in that belief, although a million miles from the right answer. The Bible defines faith as 'being sure of what we hope for and certain of what we do not see' (Hebrews 11:1). The words 'sure' and 'certain' take away any sense that biblical faith is like believing in Father Christmas even when we know it's our parents who buy the presents.

Paul, the Christian leader, used Abraham's story as an example of what faith looks like. He wrote to a large group of Christians living in Rome—the capital of the empire—setting out the basic message of the good news about Jesus. Our reading is taken from a section of the letter that teaches how Abraham was made right with God through faith.

Abraham's faith is an example for us to follow, containing four lessons:

- First, his faith was against the odds—or, as Paul expresses it, 'against all hope' (v. 18). That is a timely reminder for those of us who want answers to every question before we take a step of faith. Abraham believed God's promise that he would father a son, even though, for him and Sarah, this seemed physically impossible.
- Second, his faith kept going under pressure. We read that he didn't weaken or waver but, on the contrary, he was strengthened in his faith (v. 20). Faith is like a muscle: the more it's exercised, the stronger it becomes. Similarly, if it is never used, atrophy sets in.
- Third, his faith led him to glorify God. One of the marks of his strengthening was that Abraham was able to praise God in the long waiting period, being fully convinced that God would deliver on his promise in due time (v. 21). The waiting made him worshipful rather than consumed by anxiety.
- Fourth, his faith brought blessing. Abraham was made right with God through his faith—and, as our reading reveals, that blessing was not for him alone but for us as well. These words are written 'for us who believe' that Jesus was raised to life on Easter Day (v. 24). His death and resurrection are our source of hope and the foundation of our faith.

— Reflect —

'We today are much more fortunate than Abraham, and have little or no excuse for unbelief. For we live on this side of the resurrection. Moreover, we have a complete Bible in which both the creation of the universe and the resurrection of Jesus are recorded. It is therefore more reasonable for us to believe than it was for Abraham. Of course we have to make sure that the promises we are seeking to inherit are neither wrenched out of their biblical context nor the product of our own subjective fancy, but truly apply to us. Then we can lay hold of them, even against all human hope, yet in hope… that is, in the confidence of God's faithfulness and power. Only so shall we prove to be genuine children of our great spiritual forefather Abraham.'

JOHN R.W. STOTT[14]

✣

— 6 DECEMBER —

Faith that inherits

You are all sons of God through faith in Christ Jesus, for all of you who were baptised into Christ have clothed yourselves with Christ. There is neither Jew nor Greek, slave nor free, male nor female, for you are all one in Christ Jesus. If you belong to Christ, then you are Abraham's seed, and heirs according to the promise. What I am saying is that as long as the heir is a child, he is no different from a slave, although he owns the whole estate. He is subject to guardians and trustees until the time set by his father. So also, when we were children, we were in slavery under the basic principles of the world. But when the time had fully come, God sent his Son, born of a woman, born under law, to redeem those under law, that we might receive the full rights of sons. Because you are sons, God sent the Spirit of his Son into our hearts, the Spirit who calls out, 'Abba, Father.' So you are no longer a slave, but a son; and since you are a son, God has made you also an heir.

GALATIANS 3:26—4:7

It's the stuff of movies and novels. A relatively poor man, working in a humdrum job, is contacted by lawyers notifying him that a distant relative has died and named him in her will as sole beneficiary of a large estate. It's a rags-to-riches story of a poor man made millionaire overnight—only this is no fable; it is the essence of the gospel message.

'Poor wretches made rich' is the headline and our reading tackles the theology behind it. First Paul reveals the source of our surprise inheritance. At the right time, God sent his Son, Jesus, 'born of a woman' and 'born under the law', in order that we might receive full rights as sons. Paul is referring to the fact that Jesus kept God's law perfectly and thereby qualified as the perfect sacrifice for sin, as 'a lamb without blemish or defect' (1 Peter 1:19).

Second, Paul deals with the scope of this inheritance, which is far wider than the Jewish nation (as descendants of Abraham) was usually prepared to concede. The gospel of Christ exploded the old idea that God was only interested in one nation. Paul (as a trained rabbi) became the major exponent of this revolutionary view—and lost status and friends as a result (see Philippians 3:8). According to the gospel, everyone is eligible to inherit. There is no distinction of race ('neither Jew nor Greek'), class ('slave nor free') or gender ('male nor female') (v. 28). Those barriers that traditionally label people as insiders or outsiders are blown away in Christ.

Third, Paul writes about the sign of our inheritance, the Holy Spirit of God, who calls out within us the word 'father' in the language of deep relationship. Abba (Aramaic for 'father') was a word of family intimacy, indicating a closeness of relationship.

The way we enter into that relationship is summed up in the first sentence of our reading: 'through faith in Christ Jesus' (v. 26). Jesus is the source of our inheritance as sons and daughters of the living God. None of us is beyond the scope of this grace, and the sign that we are heirs is the presence of the Holy Spirit within us. Some of us might feel orphaned, undervalued and second-class. These words challenge such thoughts and remind us of our rich legacy.

Does our faith make us smile?

The astonishing truth that we have been adopted in God's family through Christ and made inheritors of the kingdom should fill us with joy. Rejoice today that you are an inheritor and, if you are joining others in a service of worship, thank God for the diversity and richness you observe in your sisters and brothers in the faith.

— Reflect —

'In the Baroque period the liturgy used to include the *risus paschalis*, the Easter laughter. The Easter homily had to contain a story that made people laugh, so that the church sounded with joyful laughter... Is there not something very beautiful and appropriate about laughter becoming a liturgical symbol?'

POPE BENEDICT XVI[15]

✣

— 7 DECEMBER —

Faith that loves

Therefore, although in Christ I could be bold and order you to do what you ought to do, yet I appeal to you on the basis of love. I then, as Paul—an old man and now also a prisoner of Christ Jesus—I appeal to you for my son Onesimus, who became my son while I was in chains. Formerly he was useless to you, but now he has become useful both to you and to me. I am sending him—who is my very heart—back to you. I would have liked to keep him with me so that he could take your place in helping me while I am in chains for the gospel. But I did not want to do anything without your consent, so that any favour you do will be spontaneous and not forced. Perhaps the reason he was separated from you for a little while was that you might have him back for good—no longer as a slave, but better than a slave, as a dear brother. He is very dear to me but even dearer to you, both as a man and as a brother in the Lord.

PHILEMON 8–16

There lies a lovely story behind this most personal letter contained in the New Testament. Paul (who wrote the letter) was in prison in Rome, awaiting a personal hearing before the emperor. Philemon (the man to whom the letter is addressed) was a leader of a church in the city of Colosse and the congregation met in his home. Onesimus (the main subject of the letter) was a slave in Philemon's household, who had stolen some property and run away.

Through a series of God-incidences (rather than coincidences) at which we can only guess, Onesimus crossed Paul's path and came to faith in Christ. He was useful to Paul in his situation of house arrest, but they both knew that Onesimus needed to address the implications of his previous actions. Paul sent him back to his master, Philemon, clutching this letter.

That is how a piece of private correspondence found its way into the New Testament. It's a powerful yet personal illustration of what it means to embrace a faith that loves.

For Philemon, it meant offering forgiveness and moving on. The standard punishment for runaway slaves in the Roman empire was brutal—crucifixion. A more lenient punishment was to brand the slave on the forehead, leaving him or her for ever marked as a runaway. As Paul reminds Philemon, this formerly useless slave is now not only useful,[16] but also a brother in Christ—and the new relationship carried implications.

For Onesimus, his newfound faith called him to face up to the past and live differently. Love meant paying the consequences with no guarantee of Philemon's mercy. As someone has wisely remarked, 'Christianity doesn't help someone run away from their past, but rather to face it and, by God's grace, rise above it.'

For Paul, a faith that loves meant taking a risk to be a peacemaker and taking the initiative in being a bridge-builder. He could have chosen other options—refusing to get involved or simply ordering Philemon to do as he was told—but, as our reading shows, his appeal was on the basis of love.

All three men faced the implications of a faith that, being based on love, called them to demonstrate that same love in response.

— Reflect —

This quotation from the writings of Bishop Lesslie Newbigin reminds us that a congregation is called to explain the gospel through the quality of their relationships.
(The word 'hermeneutic' means 'interpretation'.)

'I have come to feel that the primary reality of which we have to take account in seeking for a Christian impact on public life is the Christian congregation. How is it possible for the gospel to be credible, that people should come to believe that the power which has the last word in human affairs is represented by a man hanging on a cross? I am suggesting that the only answer, the only hermeneutic of the gospel, is a congregation of men and women who believe it and live by it.'[17]

How can you demonstrate a faith that loves?

8–14 DECEMBER

Promise

It is of the very essence of the Christian journey that we are storied people. Like our Jewish forefathers, we are shaped by the stories of God's actions in history. And just as the Hebrew slaves were given the enactment of the Passover and told to 'tell this to your children', so we are called to re-enact and re-tell the story of Jesus over and over. The great dramatic events of scripture tell the story of a God who time and again chooses grace over karma; who breaks into history to make losers winners; who chooses the ultimate act of self-emptying as the central drama of his own life.

GERARD KELLY[18]

We look next at several passages from the Old Testament that the first Christians understood as prophecies, which were fulfilled in Jesus Christ.

✣

— 8 DECEMBER —

Small yet significant

Marshal your troops, O city of troops, for a siege is laid against us. They will strike Israel's ruler on the cheek with a rod. 'But you, Bethlehem Ephrathah, though you are small among the clans of Judah, out of you will come for me one who will be ruler over Israel, whose origins are from of old, from ancient times.' Therefore Israel will be abandoned until the time when she who is in labour gives birth and the rest of his brothers return to join the Israelites. He will stand and shepherd his flock in the strength of the Lord, in the majesty of the name of the Lord his God. And they will live securely, for then his greatness will reach to the ends of the earth. And he will be their peace.

MICAH 5:1–5

Micah was a contemporary of Isaiah but, beyond that, little is known of him. He faithfully spoke God's message to people who had gone away from Yahweh. Much of his message concerned God's judgment on his rebellious people, but within the prophecies are glimpses of hope. Our reading contains a promise of a coming king to be born in an unlikely location—Bethlehem. The early church saw here a picture of Jesus, and this begs the question as to how much Micah understood of what he wrote.

The Christian leader Peter, writing later, suggested that the full import of the Old Testament prophets' words was somehow veiled (see 1 Peter 1:10–12), underlining our privilege in being able to marvel at the wonder of God's rescue plan for lost people.

Micah's words put Bethlehem on the map, as this small, insignificant town would become the birthplace of the ruler who was 'from ancient times' and would lead his people as their shepherd. This king's greatness would reach the farthest corners of the earth. He would not simply bring his people peace—but he himself would *be* their peace. When King Herod asked the religious experts of his day where the Messiah was to be born, they quoted Micah's prophecy, as it had become received wisdom (see Matthew 2:3–6).

We marvel at how the pregnant Mary (who lived in Nazareth, almost 100 miles away) would make an uncomfortable journey south to Bethlehem—and all because of a tax return (see Luke 2:1–6). So Jesus, who would otherwise have been born in Nazareth, was born in Bethlehem, and so fulfilled Micah's prophecy.

Bethlehem was the home of the great King David, to whom God had promised that one of his descendants would establish a kingdom that would last for ever (see 1 Chronicles 17:4–14). Hundreds of years later, the details came together in the birth of Jesus of Nazareth. Truly our God is awesome and his ways past finding out!

Despite the link with David, Bethlehem was not large—but, in God's purposes, small doesn't mean insignificant. Too often we are hemmed in by the predictable and obvious, forgetting that God repeatedly chooses to use unlikely people, works in less obvious ways and shows up in unusual places.

Anita Roddick, founder of the Body Shop, was an enterprising and determined woman. These words of hers sum up her driving ambition: 'If you think you're too small to have an impact, try going to bed with a mosquito in the room.'

How often do we limit God by our own assessment of what counts as significant? Is there a 'Bethlehem' you are in danger of overlooking?

— Reflect —

'The Lord does not look at the things man looks at. Man looks at the outward appearance, but the Lord looks at the heart.'

1 SAMUEL 16:7

Father, your ways are not my ways. Help me to gain wisdom and understanding, that I may consider all things in the light of your purposes and that I may discern what is right and do what is best. In Christ's name. Amen

✣

— 9 DECEMBER —

Darkness to light

Nevertheless, there will be no more gloom for those who were in distress. In the past he humbled the land of Zebulun and the land of Naphtali, but in the future he will honour Galilee of the Gentiles, by the way of the sea, along the Jordan—

The people walking in darkness have seen a great light; on those living in the land of the shadow of death a light has dawned. You have enlarged the nation and increased their joy; they rejoice before you as people rejoice at the harvest, as men rejoice when dividing the plunder. For as in the day of Midian's defeat, you have shattered the yoke that burdens them, the bar across their shoulders, the rod of their oppressor. Every warrior's boot used in battle and every garment rolled in blood will be destined for burning, will be fuel for the fire. For to us a child is born, to us a son is given, and the government will be on his shoulders. And he will be called Wonderful Counsellor, Mighty God, Everlasting Father, Prince of Peace. Of the increase of his government and peace there will be no end. He will reign on David's throne and over his kingdom, establishing and upholding it with justice and righteousness from that time on and forever. The zeal of the Lord Almighty will accomplish this.

ISAIAH 9:1–7

The birth of a child is an event for celebration and rejoicing. The birth of a royal child often gives even greater cause to celebrate, for a whole nation. In his prophecy, Isaiah foresaw a time when some parts of northern Israel, which had suffered under the tyrannical assaults of the Assyrians, would see a new dawn. These were 'the people who walked in darkness' for whom a new light would shine (v. 2).

In God's greater purpose, this prophecy also pointed to the coming of Jesus, who grew up in the region of Galilee and began his public preaching there. The first communicators of the Christian message made the connection with Isaiah's words (see Matthew 4:12–17).

In the Near East it was customary for a royal heir to be given 'throne names' as expressions of hope and blessing for their reign. One Egyptian monarch was called 'Lord of Justice' and 'King who Protects and Builds'. Consider the titles that are given, in our Bible passage, to this son born to reign over a kingdom that will never end.

- 'Wonderful Counsellor' speaks of his infinite wisdom, which brought the very universe into being and sustains it by his power. Jesus Christ is the source of all wisdom and understanding and the one whom we can trust with absolute confidence.
- 'Mighty God' refers to his supreme power. He is the one in whom all power and authority reside. There is simply none greater, and, as someone has wisely remarked, 'omnipotence knows no limitations'.
- 'Everlasting Father' is the throne name that speaks of his compassion and ability to provide for his people. This is a title of relationship and security within the context of family, where those who dwell are in a place of safety.
- 'Prince of Peace' reminds us of the *shalom* (wholeness) that comes from God alone and is unlike any peace on offer elsewhere (see John 14:27).

Wisdom, power, compassion and peace are the throne names of Jesus. For those who celebrate his coming and choose to live under his rule and authority, these names are fuel for wonder, praise and worship.

— Reflect —

Spend some moments thinking about these throne names and offer your praise and worship to King Jesus. Then consider the things that trouble you and act on this promise:

Let us then approach the throne of grace with confidence, so that we may receive mercy and find grace to help us in our time of need (Hebrews 4:16).

✣

— 10 DECEMBER —

Opposed but victorious

Why do the nations conspire and the peoples plot in vain? The kings of the earth take their stand and the rulers gather together against the Lord and against his Anointed One. 'Let us break their chains,' they say, 'and throw off their fetters.' The One enthroned in heaven laughs; the Lord scoffs at them. Then he rebukes them in his anger and terrifies them in his wrath, saying, 'I have installed my King on Zion, my holy hill.' I will proclaim the decree of the Lord: He said to me, 'You are my Son; today I have become your Father. Ask of me, and I will make the nations your inheritance, the ends of the earth your possession. You will rule them with an iron sceptre; you will dash them to pieces like pottery.' Therefore, you kings, be wise; be warned, you rulers of the earth. Serve the Lord with fear and rejoice with trembling. Kiss the Son, lest he be angry and you be destroyed in your way, for his wrath can flare up in a moment. Blessed are all who take refuge in him.

PSALM 2

Imagine being arrested by the authorities, threatened with dire consequences if you continued practising your faith and then being thrown out on the street. Many fellow believers face this type of harassment, and worse, on a daily basis.

Two leaders of the early Church faced such a situation and, on their release from prison, they gathered their supporters for a time of prayer (see Acts 4:23–31). As often happens when people pray, a passage of scripture was quoted that seemed to fit the circumstances and add understanding to what was happening.

The passage quoted comes from today's reading, Psalm 2. This psalm, originally used in the coronation ceremony for a new king, had become connected with Israel's hope that Yahweh's anointed one (or 'Messiah') would one day come.

It starts with a question: why are the nations resisting Yahweh and his anointed one? The Lord laughs at such futile attempts to resist his purpose, which will be accomplished through his Son. This Son's inheritance will be more than the land promised to Abraham: it will be the very nations of the world. Those who are wise will not resist but will rather worship him.

The first Christians, when faced with the hostile reaction of the religious authorities, took hope from the big picture of God's great purpose. They saw their story in the context of God's bigger story. Bishop Tom Wright expresses it well:

When the apostles quote Psalm 2 in their confident, exhilarated prayer... they are not just finding a vague proof-text to help them anchor a general sense that all the world is against them. They are calling up a very specific text which speaks graphically and powerfully of the Messiah as the son of God, destined to rule the whole world... Praying like this is confident praying, not because people necessarily feel more devout than at other times, but because they are rooting themselves firmly in the ancient tradition of scripture.[19]

There are some lessons here for us. First, God's greater purpose should always be our focus, as Jesus taught in the opening section of the Disciple's Prayer (better known as the Lord's Prayer): 'Your kingdom come, your will be done' (Matthew 6:10). Second, we are reminded of the importance of perspective in respect of our own circumstances. Peter and John didn't ask God to punish the authorities or even change their minds, rather that they themselves would be bold and strong in doing what God wanted them to do. Third, we see again the vital importance of prayer—not only for ourselves but also for those who pay a high price for a faith that we sometimes treat cheaply.

— Focus —

If you have access to the Internet, look up Christian Solidarity Worldwide (www.csw.org.uk) and Open Doors (www.opendoorsuk.org), two organizations providing information about the persecuted church.

Pray for those who suffer for their faith, that they may know God's strength through the encouragement of the scriptures.

✣

— 11 DECEMBER —

New and better

'The time is coming,' declares the Lord, 'when I will make a new covenant with the house of Israel and with the house of Judah. It will not be like the covenant I made with their forefathers when I took them by the hand to lead them out of Egypt, because they broke my covenant, though I was a husband to them,' declares the Lord. 'This is the covenant I will make with the house of Israel after that time,' declares the Lord. 'I will put my law in their minds and write it on their hearts. I will be their God, and they will be my people. No longer will a man teach his neighbour, or a man his brother, saying, 'Know the Lord,' because they will all know me, from the least of them to the greatest,' declares the Lord. 'For I will forgive their wickedness and will remember their sins no more.'

JEREMIAH 31:31–34

Jeremiah was a tender man called to a tough task. He was a priest, called by God to deliver an uncomfortable message of judgment to the people of Judah—a role that he faithfully fulfilled for 40 years. He trod a lonely path with few friends and, according to some sources, was eventually stoned to death by his own countrymen. The depth of his sorrow is apparent in his writings and has given him the title of 'the weeping prophet'.

Our reading, however, shows Jeremiah looking further ahead than his own generation to a time when God would make a new covenant to replace the old one given through Moses, which was stubbornly and consistently broken by his rebellious people.

The first Christians saw this prophecy as being fulfilled in Jesus Christ, and the writer to the Hebrews quotes Jeremiah's promise in full (see Hebrews 8:8–12), making this the longest quotation from the Old Testament in the New. But what makes this covenant new and how does it differ from the old?

In answer to the second part of the question, one writer summarises the status of the old covenant, once Jesus had come, as 'imperfect, powerless and obsolete'.[20] As to the new covenant, Jeremiah pinpoints no fewer than five outstanding features, which are foundational to our understanding of the Christian faith.

- Unity: The houses of Judah and Israel are mentioned separately because, in Jeremiah's time, the nation was divided as a result of civil war. The new covenant, however, would reunite divided people.
- Inward: The old covenant included laws written down at first on stone tablets and later in scrolls; under the new one, God's laws would be internalised in heart and mind.
- Everyone: The new covenant would not be confined to teachers and experts or those with wealth or status. 'They will all know me, from the least of them to the greatest' (v. 34) is the astonishing promise.
- Forgiveness: Here is hope for wicked and rebellious people. Somehow, this new covenant would make forgiveness possible: a fresh start with a clean slate was on offer.
- Guaranteed: Look back through today's reading and note the number of times the words 'I will' are used. This is more than slick advertising jargon. The new covenant is made by God himself, based on the rock-solid guarantee of his character.

This new covenant is better in every way, but we are left with the question as to how it can be possible. The words of our Lord Jesus at the last supper provide the answer: as he took the cup and offered it to his disciples, he said, 'This cup is the new covenant in my blood, which is poured out for you' (Luke 22:20).

— Reflect —

Each time we share in Holy Communion, we are reminded of the new covenant made possible through the sacrifice of Jesus Christ. Thank God—Father, Son and Spirit—for such love.

Amazing Grace, how sweet the sound
That saved a wretch like me.
I once was lost, but now am found,
Was blind, but now I see.

JOHN NEWTON (1725–1807)

✣

— 12 DECEMBER —

Free, not cheap

Who has believed our message and to whom has the arm of the Lord been revealed? He grew up before him like a tender shoot, and like a root out of dry ground. He had no beauty or majesty to attract us to him, nothing in his appearance that we should desire him. He was despised and rejected by men, a man of sorrows, and familiar with suffering. Like one from whom men hide their faces he was despised, and we esteemed him not. Surely he took up our infirmities and carried our sorrows, yet we considered him stricken by God, smitten by him, and afflicted. But he was pierced for our transgressions, he was crushed for our iniquities; the punishment that brought us peace was upon him, and by his wounds we are healed. We all, like sheep, have gone astray, each of us has turned to his own way; and the Lord has laid on him the iniquity of us all.

ISAIAH 53:1–6

If you have ever been stuck and someone has come to your rescue, you will know something of the deep sense of gratitude that we feel in such a situation.

There was a man who held a high-powered job, yet lived with a gnawing sense that life had more to offer. He set off on a quest that took him far from home and led him to some strange people. He saw their way of life and the religion that shaped them and, before returning home, bought a book by one of their revered thinkers. The problem was that it was written in another language and, for all his education, the man could not understand what the writer was trying to say. Then, out of the blue, on his journey home, a fellow traveller turned up who made the whole thing clearer.

The story of this strange encounter is found in the New Testament book of Acts (see 8:26–40). Although we know little about the man, there is a strong tradition that he returned to his homeland of Ethiopia as a contagious follower of Jesus who wasted no time in sharing the good news that had changed his life.

The link between today's reading and that incident is this: the Ethiopian man was struggling to understand this very chapter of Isaiah. The one who helped him make sense of it was Philip, a man who went on to become a notable communicator of the Christian message. Dr Luke (who wrote Acts as volume 2 of his Gospel) reports, 'Then Philip began with that very passage of Scripture [Isaiah 53] and told him the good news about Jesus' (Acts 8:35).

Writing centuries earlier, Isaiah had painted a picture of a suffering servant who would accomplish God's will. Israel as a nation had been chosen by God to be a light to the other nations, but had failed. Through prayer and deep thought, Isaiah saw a picture of one who would come and complete the task, bearing the burden not only of Israel's sin but also that of the whole of humankind.

Isaiah set out the job description and the first Christians declared that Jesus fitted the bill completely. Consider the portrait: here is a man described as so unattractive that people can't bear to look at him, despised, rejected and someone who lives with suffering. Words such as 'stricken', 'smitten', 'afflicted', 'pierced', 'crushed', 'punishment' and 'wounds' convey the opposite of a conquering king. But here is one who stoops to conquer. We are the straying sheep, the sinful rebels; he is the one willing to die as a substitute, bearing 'the iniquity of us all' (v. 6).

One of the early Church Fathers, Cyril of Alexandria, wrote of Isaiah's suffering servant that God himself 'became a beggar on earth, in order that we might become rich from his poverty'.[21]

Grace is free—but not cheap.

— Reflect —

Death and darkness, get you packing,
Nothing now to man is lacking.
All your triumphs now are ended,
And what Adam marred is mended.

HENRY VAUGHAN (1621–95)

✣

— 13 DECEMBER —

Gentle, not weak

'Here is my servant, whom I uphold, my chosen one in whom I delight; I will put my Spirit on him and he will bring justice to the nations. He will not shout or cry out, or raise his voice in the streets. A bruised reed he will not break, and a smouldering wick he will not snuff out. In faithfulness he will bring forth justice; he will not falter or be discouraged till he establishes justice on earth. In his law the islands will put their hope.' This is what God the Lord says—he who created the heavens and stretched them out, who spread out the earth and all that comes out of it, who gives breath to its people, and life to those who walk on it: 'I, the Lord, have called you in righteousness; I will take hold of your hand. I will keep you and will make you to be a covenant for the people and a light for the Gentiles, to open eyes that are blind, to free captives from prison and to release from the dungeon those who sit in darkness.'

ISAIAH 42:1–7

Here is another description of Isaiah's servant, the one who will fulfil Yahweh's purpose. The servant is chosen by the Lord to bring justice 'to the nations' (v. 1): notice that this mission extends beyond Israel. Isaiah describes a person who possesses quiet strength, tenderness and faithfulness, a servant who will establish justice on the earth. We are safe in his hands.

When Matthew came to write his account of Jesus, he knew that his first readers would be like himself, from the background of the Jewish faith. Sensitive to this, he includes a large number of references to passages from the Old Testament to make the point that Jesus fulfilled what God had long promised.

Matthew quotes today's passage when he reports the healing ministry of Jesus (see 12:15–21). Crowds came, bringing relatives and friends who were ill, Matthew records, 'and he healed all their sick' (v. 15). These miracles were signs of the kingdom that had arrived, through the coming of Jesus, into the world. They pointed to the future kingdom when all sickness, death, evil and sin will be finally eradicated (see Revelation 21:4).

What Matthew and his fellow preachers identified in Jesus of Nazareth was a living demonstration of what Isaiah had described centuries before.

- 'A bruised reed' conveys a picture of tall grass bent double by the wind, damaged beyond hope of repair. The skilful gardener, with gentle touch, is able to straighten the grass without breaking it, and binds a stake in place, enabling the plant to grow strong.
- 'A smouldering wick' is a picture of a candle about to be extinguished in a draught of wind. It splutters in a final act before the death of its fading light. The hands of God's servant gather and shield the delicate wick, allowing the flame to rekindle and catch light strongly once more.

These are pictures of God's grace at work. There is no harsh criticism or rigid rules, no words of condemnation designed to break spirits that are already damaged enough. From Jesus come words of hope and hands of healing.

The first prayer I learned as a child began, 'Gentle Jesus, meek and mild...' and I am grateful to God for a loving mother who taught me to pray it, but it has taken me most of my life to understand what it means. Even now I would not claim to have grasped it fully, but I do know that meekness should never be confused with weakness. The late Professor William Barclay described it as 'controlled strength'.[22]

The hands of Jesus are safe and they heal.

— Reflect —

Are there areas of your life that are bruised or smouldering?
Do you know someone who needs the safe hands of Jesus?
Spend some moments in prayer.

Lord Jesus Christ, as I bring these needs to you and place them in your hands, grant, in your mercy, healing grace. In your name. Amen

✣

— 14 DECEMBER —

Rejected yet chosen

Open for me the gates of righteousness; I will enter and give thanks to the Lord. This is the gate of the Lord through which the righteous may enter. I will give you thanks, for you answered me; you have become my salvation. The stone the builders rejected has become the capstone; the Lord has done this, and it is marvellous in our eyes. This is the day the Lord has made; let us rejoice and be glad in it. O Lord, save us; O Lord, grant us success. Blessed is he who comes in the name of the Lord. From the house of the Lord we bless you.

PSALM 118:19–26

This psalm contains verses quoted more than once in the New Testament, most significantly by Jesus. He believed that the stone rejected by the builders referred to himself (see Matthew 21:42). The early church agreed, and two of their leaders quoted it at their trial in a top religious court.

The writer of this psalm was probably referring either to a king of Israel or to the nation itself, looked down upon and treated with contempt by neighbouring peoples. The 'capstone' was a stone used to anchor and align the corner of a wall, or sometimes as a load-bearing lintel above a door. The Hebrew word for 'corner' was often used as a word picture for a leader, one who holds things together. (We sometimes talk of someone, similarly, as a 'pillar of the community'.) The point of the metaphor is that the builders rejected this stone and left it lying in the corner of the yard, but the Lord himself took the rejected stone and made it the most important in his building project.

The stone is Jesus, and the builders are the religious leaders who rejected his authority, maligned his character and eventually handed him over to be crucified.

Peter boldly asserted, before the very court that had condemned his Lord, that they were the 'expert' builders who had rejected the capstone (see Acts 4:11). We can only imagine the effect that this stinging rebuke would have had on men who knew their Old Testament scriptures so well.

The 'capstone' of Psalm 118 is sometimes linked with Isaiah's description of 'a stone that causes men to stumble and a rock that makes them fall' (Isaiah 8:14). The religious leaders of Jesus' day 'fell over' a Messiah who didn't fit their expectations and a God who wasn't acting in the way they wanted. Still today, Jesus is a stumbling block to some (because he is inconvenient), yet a stepping stone to others (who find in him truth, grace and love).

Expectations play an important part in our experience of faith, and our understanding of who Jesus is plays a fundamental part. Do we try to make him fit our expectations or do we allow our expectations to be shaped by the revelation of Christ given us in the Bible?

American author Donald Miller has written extensively about his faith journey. He struggled with the false expectations produced by 'How to...' sermons, formulas for 'a victorious life' and people who offered 'three steps to success'. He writes of his liberating discovery:

The truth is there are a million steps, and we don't even know what the steps are, and worse, at any given moment we may not be willing or even able to take them; and still worse, they are different for you and me and they are always changing. I have come to believe the sooner we find this truth beautiful, the sooner we will fall in love with the God who keeps shaking things up, keeps changing the path, keeps rocking the boat to test our faith in Him, teaching us not to rely on easy answers, bullet points, magic mantras or genies in lamps, but rather in His guidance, His existence, His mercy, and His love.[23]

— Reflect —

Open my eyes that I may see wonderful things in your law.

PSALM 119:18

Lord, open my eyes that I may see you and understand your ways.
Transform my expectations, reshape my values and be my vision.
Amen

15–21 DECEMBER

Encounter

Here is The Story, the grand universal narrative that stretches from creation to new creation, and accounts for everything in between. This is The Story that tells us where we have come from, how we got to be here, who we are, why the world is in the mess it is, how it can be (and has been) changed, and where we are ultimately going. And the whole story is predicated on the reality of God and the mission of this God. He is the originator of the story, the teller of the story, the prime actor in the story, the planner and guide of the story's plot, the meaning of the story and its ultimate completion. He is its beginning, end and centre. It is the story of the mission of God, of this God and no other.

CHRISTOPHER WRIGHT[24]

Our next readings examine stories of those who encountered God in surprising ways.

✣

— 15 DECEMBER —

Deeper in the grass

When it was time for Elizabeth to have her baby, she gave birth to a son. Her neighbours and relatives heard that the Lord had shown her great mercy, and they shared her joy. On the eighth day they came to circumcise the child, and they were going to name him after his father Zechariah, but his mother spoke up and said, 'No! He is to be called John.' They said to her, 'There is no one among your relatives who has that name.' Then they made signs to his father, to find out what he would like to name the child. He asked for a writing tablet, and to everyone's astonishment he wrote, 'His name is John.' Immediately his mouth was opened and his tongue was loosed, and he began to speak, praising God. The neighbours were all filled with awe, and throughout the hill country of Judea people were talking about all these things. Everyone who heard this wondered about it, asking, 'What then is this child going to be?' For the Lord's hand was with him.

LUKE 1:57–66

Familiarity, they say, breeds contempt. That may be a sweeping generalization but most of us recognise the risk of taking for granted whatever is familiar.

Zechariah was the father of John the Baptist and our reading describes the birth of this unexpected child. Zechariah and his wife, Elizabeth, had been unable to have children and were both well on in years, so news of the pregnancy brought a mixture of shock and joy. The announcement was also most unusual as, in this case, the father knew about it before the mother (see Luke 1:5–25).

Zechariah was a priest, chosen to offer incense in the inner sanctuary of the temple. This was a privilege allowed only once in a priest's career: some were never chosen by lot, so this day was a once-in-a-lifetime experience for Zechariah.

It was made even more memorable, though, when an angel announced that a special child was to be born to Zechariah and his wife. Zechariah did not believe the promise at first and so was rendered unable to speak until the baby was born. Our reading records the confusion surrounding the naming of the child: people were puzzled by his mother's refusal to follow custom and name him after a relative. Zechariah's insistence that he should be called John was significant: this was the name that had been given by the angel months earlier, and an acknowledgment that God had kept his word.

As a priest, Zechariah was a man of faith, charged with nurturing faith in others. Yet when his faith was tested by God, he failed.

At a recent Sunday service, we were challenged by the preacher to think of the ways in which we are deaf and blind and in need of Christ's healing touch. During the quiet period of reflection at the end of the service, I realised once again the dangers attached to being familiar with holy things. It is all too easy to become lifeless in the routines of faith, to settle for comfort rather than risk, and to be content with the predictable.

Zechariah probably preached to others about encountering God; he just hadn't expected God to transform *his* life. What does that say to us about faith that expects and believes?

— Reflect —

In his poem 'The Chapel', Welsh poet R.S. Thomas reminds us of the danger of settling 'a little deeper into the grass':

A little aside from the main road
becalmed in last-century greyness
there is the chapel, ugly, without the appeal

to the tourist to stop his car
and visit it. The traffic goes by,
and the river goes by, and quick shadows
of clouds too, and the chapel settles
a little deeper into the grass.

But here once on an evening like this
in the darkness that was about
his hearers, a preacher caught fire
and burned steadily before them
with a strange light, so that they saw
the splendour of the barren mountains
about them and sang their amens
fiercely, narrow but saved
in a way that men are not now.[25]

✣

— 16 DECEMBER —

A believing believer

In the sixth month, God sent the angel Gabriel to Nazareth, a town in Galilee, to a virgin pledged to be married to a man named Joseph, a descendant of David. The virgin's name was Mary. The angel went to her and said, 'Greetings, you who are highly favoured! The Lord is with you.' Mary was greatly troubled at his words and wondered what kind of greeting this might be. But the angel said to her, 'Do not be afraid, Mary, you have found favour with God. You will be with child and give birth to a son, and you are to give him the name Jesus. He will be great and will be called the Son of the Most High. The Lord God will give him the throne of his father David, and he will reign over the house of Jacob forever; his kingdom will never end.' 'How will this be,' Mary asked the angel, 'since I am a virgin?' The angel answered, 'The Holy Spirit will come upon you, and the power of the Most High will overshadow you. So the holy one to be born will be called the Son of God. Even Elizabeth your relative is going to have a child in her old age, and she who was said to be barren is in her sixth month. For nothing is impossible with God.' 'I am the Lord's servant,' Mary answered. 'May it be to me as you have said.' Then the angel left her.

LUKE 1:26–38

Around the time of Christ's birth, women experienced a hard life. One of the six major divisions of the Mishna (the collection of Jewish religious laws) is devoted exclusively to rules about women, including 72 paragraphs concerning ritual uncleanness and menstruation. A woman had no identity or place in public life, she had no right of divorce and was effectively a slave in her own home. She was not allowed to pray at a meal table or give evidence in court because women were generally considered to be liars. They could not study the law of Moses, let alone teach it, and were restricted in their access to parts of the temple or synagogue. No wonder men prayed daily, 'Blessed be God that hath not made me a woman.'[26]

All of this makes it truly remarkable that Yahweh, Israel's God, should single out a teenage girl from a humble home to carry his Son in her womb.

It seems a deliberate choice on Luke's part to draw a contrast between Zechariah's response to the angel Gabriel (Luke 1:18: 'How can I be sure of this?') and that of Mary. Zechariah was a man, a priest, advanced in years and respected; Mary was young, a woman, with no status in the public eye. The great distinction is seen is their faith—or, in Zechariah's case, the lack of it. They both asked questions, but what lay behind the questions revealed what was in their hearts.

Mary was understandably shocked to receive the news and Luke notes that she was greatly troubled and afraid. But when she asked how it would be possible for a virgin to conceive, she was told, 'Nothing is impossible with God' (v. 37). Luke records her humble and obedient response, which would be echoed by her Son in his prayer in the garden called Gethsemane 34 years later: 'Yet not my will, but yours be done' (Luke 22:42).

The contrast between experienced Zechariah and young Mary helps us to recognise that spiritual maturity has little to do with job titles and qualifications and much more to do with the state of our hearts.

What lessons can we draw from Mary's example of uncomplicated faith and unhesitating obedience?

— Reflect —

'By word and deed Jesus confers a new dignity on women. One confesses him as Lord. He reveals his messianic nature to another.

And women, of all people, are chosen as the first witnesses of the resurrection. In a male dominated culture these were powerful signs that women had a new status in the upside down kingdom.'

DONALD KRAYBILL[27]

What other examples can you give of the 'upside down kingdom'? How should they shape our values and choices?

✣

— 17 DECEMBER —

Hidden hero

This is how the birth of Jesus Christ came about: His mother Mary was pledged to be married to Joseph, but before they came together, she was found to be with child through the Holy Spirit. Because Joseph her husband was a righteous man and did not want to expose her to public disgrace, he had in mind to divorce her quietly. But after he had considered this, an angel of the Lord appeared to him in a dream and said, 'Joseph son of David, do not be afraid to take Mary home as your wife, because what is conceived in her is from the Holy Spirit. She will give birth to a son, and you are to give him the name Jesus, because he will save his people from their sins.' All this took place to fulfil what the Lord had said through the prophet, 'The virgin will be with child and will give birth to a son, and they will call him Immanuel'—which means, 'God with us'. When Joseph woke up, he did what the angel of the Lord commanded him and took Mary home as his wife. But he had no union with her until she gave birth to a son. And he gave him the name Jesus.

MATTHEW 1:18–25

I have been privileged to know some hidden heroes. They are people who avoid the limelight and never make the headlines, yet, in their own quiet, unassuming way, they make the world go round. You probably know some too.

Joseph was one such hero. In nativity plays, he is often relegated to standing and watching the proceedings, but in fact he was a key player, not an extra.

Matthew records Joseph's betrothal to Mary. There would have been a twelve-month period of betrothal leading up to the marriage ceremony. This was more formal than a modern-day engagement because part of the bride price would have been paid and any last-minute change of mind would entail formal divorce proceedings. Mary would have been between 12 and 14, and Joseph between 18 and 20 years of age, and their respective families would have arranged the marriage. Behind such details, however, we read of God's hand at work.

When Joseph discovered that Mary was pregnant, there could be only one conclusion: she had been unfaithful in her year of betrothal. But Joseph (described as 'a righteous man', v. 19) didn't want his pound of flesh, in spite of the inevitable feelings of betrayal. He wanted the circumstances kept quiet—especially for Mary's sake, it seems. Notice, it was *after* he had made this decision that an angel arrived with an astonishing announcement. Mary had not been unfaithful—far from it. Her faithfulness had qualified her in heaven's eyes to carry the one who would be Saviour of the world.

How did Joseph respond to the news that the child being carried by Mary was a miraculous work of the Spirit? We are told that he carried on with life as normal, yet honoured her by not having sexual relations until after the birth of Jesus.

It is easy to skate over these verses and forget that Joseph had to live in a real community, surrounded by friends and family who would draw their own conclusions. In their minds (and doubtless their gossip), there were only two possibilities: either Joseph had jumped the gun by having sex before he should have, or Mary had been sleeping around. Either way, a cloud of shame would hang low over both of them. For Joseph, living in a macho culture, life would have become very uncomfortable.

Three lessons stand out from the life of this hidden hero: maturity, flexibility and stickability. Maturity led Joseph to be entrusted with great responsibility, flexibility meant he could live with the scandal, and stickability showed that he was committed. Such a life requires strong roots.

— Reflect —

'There's a view… that in an age like ours, of unprecedented change, our values, too, must change… It's a view that couldn't be more wrong. It's when the winds blow hardest that you need the deepest roots. When you're entering uncharted territory, it's when you need a compass to give you a sense of direction.'

CHIEF RABBI SIR JONATHAN SACKS[28]

✣

— 18 DECEMBER —

Outsiders to insiders

And there were shepherds living out in the fields nearby, keeping watch over their flocks at night. An angel of the Lord appeared to them, and the glory of the Lord shone around them, and they were terrified. But the angel said to them, 'Do not be afraid. I bring you good news of great joy that will be for all the people. Today in the town of David a Saviour has been born to you; he is Christ the Lord. This will be a sign to you: You will find a baby wrapped in cloths and lying in a manger.' Suddenly a great company of the heavenly host appeared with the angel, praising God and saying, 'Glory to God in the highest, and on earth peace to men on whom his favour rests.' When the angels had left them and gone into heaven, the shepherds said to one another, 'Let's go to Bethlehem and see this thing that has happened, which the Lord has told us about.'

LUKE 2:8–15

Whenever I read about the shepherds in the Gospels, my mind is transported to numerous school halls and the sight of children in dressing-gowns, wearing tea towels on their heads and carrying toy sheep under their arms.

Such memories can cloud the real picture, though. Here were a bunch of working-class men facing some unexpected trouble on the night shift, which led to an experience they probably never forgot (or stopped talking about) for the rest of their lives.

Shepherds were, in many ways, excluded. Their job was menial and the religious élite despised them for it, which meant that they came close to bottom in the social pecking order. It is therefore surprising—some would say, shocking—that they were privileged guests in the front row at an angelic choir performance of a lifetime. When the Son of God was born as a man, heaven simply couldn't keep quiet, but it wasn't a performance held at the Jerusalem temple before a select audience of religious bigwigs. This was 'angels unplugged' on a hillside outside Bethlehem—in front of a bunch of nobodies.

Luke appears to be making the point that the shepherds were, by God's grace, included. Notice, in our reading, the impact of their night-time encounter on this group of anonymous farm workers, and the way it changed them.

At first, they were fearful—which is hardly surprising, given the circumstances. Luke uses the word 'terrified' (v. 9), strongly suggesting that this was more than a passing moment of mild upset. Fear turned to astonishment as they heard an incredible announcement about the Messiah being born in Bethlehem, just a short distance away. They were given a bizarre sign to look out for: a baby in cattle a trough. Then came the angelic choir, which must have lifted them to a level of experience that defied description.

Having seen for themselves that the child had indeed been born, the shepherds became contagious in spreading the news to everyone they met. Our last glimpse of them conveys sheer joy as they praised God for all he had done. This was a day of good news and great joy.

I wonder what happened in the days, months and years that followed. Did some of the shepherds live long enough to see the man Jesus, hear his teaching and witness the miracles? Or did they die wondering what would become of the child that had made the heavens sing '*Gloria in excelsis Deo*'?

They certainly would never have forgotten the words of the angel, 'I bring you good news', because, on that dark night in the Bethlehem hills, a light shone, turning outsiders into insiders.

It's called grace—outrageous grace. And it's free.

— Reflect —

My heart rejoices in the Lord...
There is no one holy like the Lord;
there is no one besides you;
there is no Rock like our God...
He raises the poor from the dust
and lifts the needy from the ash heap;
he seats them with princes
and has them inherit a throne of honour.

ADAPTED FROM HANNAH'S SONG (1 SAMUEL 2:1–10)

✣

— 19 DECEMBER —

Seekers become finders

Then Herod called the Magi secretly and found out from them the exact time the star had appeared. He sent them to Bethlehem and said, 'Go and make a careful search for the child. As soon as you find him, report to me, so that I too may go and worship him.' After they had heard the king, they went on their way, and the star they had seen in the east went ahead of them until it stopped over the place where the child was. When they saw the star, they were overjoyed. On coming to the house, they saw the child with his mother Mary, and they bowed down and worshipped him. Then they opened their treasures and presented him with gifts of gold and of incense and of myrrh. And having been warned in a dream not to go back to Herod, they returned to their country by another route.

MATTHEW 2:7–12

Who were these strange travellers and what made them make a long journey to a foreign country in search of a baby?

The lack of precise information available to us has led to a build-up of legend and myth, but there are no reliable grounds for claiming that there were three of them, that we know their names and that they were kings. Probably the closest we can get to the truth is that they were astrologers who studied the skies and came from somewhere close to modern-day Iran. Something they had noticed in the heavens set them searching and asking questions.

The astonishing thing is that they came as Gentiles to honour the birth of a Jewish king, bringing with them costly gifts as a mark of respect. Their first port of call was logical—the royal palace of Herod the Great in Jerusalem. But Herod was an evil, paranoid man who had murdered close family members in a ruthless bid to stay in power. The mention of a new king spread panic in the palace and beyond (Matthew 2:3), and Herod extracted as much information as he could from his religious experts before sending the foreign visitors away with strict instructions to keep him informed (v. 8). The lethal irony in Herod's stated intention to 'worship' this new king is contained in the word itself. It is made up of two Greek words meaning 'to draw near to kiss'—but Herod's true intention was to kill.

It is likely that these events took place many months after the birth of Jesus, as Matthew's reference to their entering the house (v. 11) dispels the picture of a typical nativity play scene with shepherds and wise men side by side. Significantly, however, they bowed down, worshipped and offered their precious gifts. Babies can and do prompt strange responses from adults, but this reaction was something else. This was holy ground.

These curious pilgrims found what they were looking for and, on receiving some supernatural safety advice (v. 12), slipped from the story as quietly as they had entered it.

Many have reflected on the faith, energy, devotion and sheer doggedness of these travellers. A Christian leader of a previous generation summed up the challenge presented by their faith:

They saw no miracles to convince them. They heard no teaching to persuade them. They saw no signs of divinity or greatness to overawe them. We read of no greater faith than this in the whole volume of the Bible. It is a faith that deserves to be placed side by side with that of the penitent thief. Blessed indeed are those who believe in this way![29]

— Reflect —

'I find their faith, their insight, their wholehearted search and adoring worship utterly amazing. It is one of the many surprises in the Gospel. But then God is the God of surprises. Those who think they can predict his actions need to think again. How sad that in many churches, this element of surprise is almost entirely absent, and boring predictability governs all that happens!'

MICHAEL GREEN[30]

What do these men teach us? How are their wisdom and devotion demonstrated? Are we open for the God of surprises to show us new things?

✣

— 20 DECEMBER —

Watching and waiting

Now there was a man in Jerusalem called Simeon, who was righteous and devout. He was waiting for the consolation of Israel, and the Holy Spirit was upon him. It had been revealed to him by the Holy Spirit that he would not die before he had seen the Lord's Christ. Moved by the Spirit, he went into the temple courts. When the parents brought in the child Jesus to do for him what the custom of the Law required, Simeon took him in his arms and praised God, saying: 'Sovereign Lord, as you have promised, you now dismiss your servant in peace. For my eyes have seen your salvation, which you have prepared in the sight of all people, a light for revelation to the Gentiles and for glory to your people Israel.' The child's father and mother marvelled at what was said about him. Then Simeon blessed them and said to Mary, his mother: 'This child is destined to cause the falling and rising of many in Israel, and to be a sign that will be spoken against, so that the thoughts of many hearts will be revealed. And a sword will pierce your own soul too.'

LUKE 2:25–35

We considered yesterday that we worship a God of surprises, and our reading today develops that theme.

Mary and Joseph were surprised by a complete stranger taking their baby in his arms, and uttering some words that they were probably unable to understand fully. They had gone to the temple after the regulatory 40 days had passed to offer the necessary sacrifice following childbirth. It was here that they met Simeon.

With characteristic efficiency, Dr Luke provides five key pieces of information about this man.

- His home was in Jerusalem.
- He was good and devout.
- He was waiting for the Messiah to come.
- The Holy Spirit rested on him.
- He was living with a promise.

The final point about the promise is most important, as this was the day when it would be fulfilled. God had somehow told Simeon that he would not die until he had seen the long-awaited Messiah with his own eyes. On this particular day, the Spirit told him to go to the temple at the very time when Joseph and Mary were going there.

Simeon took the young baby Jesus in his arms and uttered words that have become known and sung the world over for centuries. Simeon's song is often known by its Latin title, *Nunc Dimittis*, and it is rich with faith, thanksgiving and promise. (Have you noticed how many songs surround the birth of Jesus?)[31]

As Simeon handed back the baby, he blessed Joseph and Mary and spoke more words that, in time, were fulfilled. Jesus did grow to become a point of division between those who accepted and those who rejected him, and Mary would know the heart-piercing grief of seeing her son dying, crucified, in public humiliation.

Although we can't be certain, tradition suggests that Simeon was an elderly man when this encounter occurred, and it could well have been that he had carried the promise of God in his heart for many years.

We live in an instant generation, where we expect to be able to connect a phone call in seconds, receive a reply to an email in minutes and fly to the other side of the world in hours. We do not 'do' patience well.

Simeon is a good role model for those of us who find it hard to sit still. His waiting had made him more watchful, not less, and his patient faith was rewarded. He was ready to move on to God's next chapter with a heart full of peace.

— Reflect —

Paul, the Christian leader, wrote, 'I have learned to be content whatever the circumstances. I know what it is to be in need, and I know what it is to have plenty… I can do everything through him who gives me strength' (Philippians 4:11–13).

Are you more patient than you used to be? Have you learned the secret of being content?

✣

— 21 DECEMBER —

Old but not useless

There was also a prophetess, Anna, the daughter of Phanuel, of the tribe of Asher. She was very old; she had lived with her husband seven years after her marriage, and then was a widow until she was eighty-four. She never left the temple but worshipped night and day, fasting and praying. Coming up to them at that very moment, she gave thanks to God and spoke about the child to all who were looking forward to the redemption of Jerusalem. When Joseph and Mary had done everything required by the Law of the Lord, they returned to Galilee to their own town of Nazareth. And the child grew and became strong; he was filled with wisdom, and the grace of God was upon him.

LUKE 2:36–40

Luke turns from Simeon—an old man who had a long wait—to introduce Anna, who was an elderly woman with a big heart. Luke had a keen eye for detail (perhaps because he was a doctor) and describes Anna's life in a few lines.

We are told her father's name and tribe and the fact that she possessed the spiritual gift of prophecy. She was very old, although there is some argument over the text in verse 37 (see NIV margin): either she was married for seven years and then lived as a widow until she was 84 years old or she had been a widow for 84 years—which, by my maths, would put her at over 100 years of age.

In any case, the temple had become her life and she would have been a well-known figure there. We read of a woman of prayer and devotion—probably seen by some as a bit odd—but she is also described as a prophetess (v. 36), suggesting that people looked to her to bring God's guidance. The name Anna means 'gracious' and it seems that she lived up to the description. Her long life had been spent as an agent of grace.

Anna approached Mary and Joseph and began to give spontaneous praise to God. The description that follows suggests that there was much more here than just an elderly woman excitedly cuddling a baby. She began to speak to people 'who were looking forward to the redemption of Jerusalem' (v. 38), which would appear to be (like Simeon's declaration) a direct reference to the messianic hope of the Jewish nation.

Luke makes some important points in the early part of his book: angels, shepherds and two strangers who were people of spiritual repute all testified that here, in Jesus, was a truly special child, unlike any other. The scene closes with the family returning to the obscurity of northern Galilee, where Jesus grew up with his Father's favour on him.

Anna, like Simeon, reminds us of several important areas of life in which our generation seems to have grown careless.

- Stars and spotlights: We live in a 'celebrity culture', where some people are famous for no other reason than that they are famous. As followers of Christ, we are challenged not to be swept up in a world that has turned its values upside down. Anna and Simeon would never make the A, B or C guest list at a celebrity party today but, in heaven's opinion (the one that counts), they rank as stars.
- Age and ability: Those who believe that 'old' equals 'useless' are silenced by the story of this elderly pair of prophets. The records of the Bible and history in general reveal that some great achievers come late to the game. Within our local churches we need to honour age and welcome the wisdom of those who have been around longer than most.
- Wanting and waiting: Some of us have clung to promises from God for many, many years, and it can be disheartening when we hear of other great answers to prayer. Simeon and Anna are patron

saints for those who sit in the waiting room while everyone else's number gets called!

— Reflect —

Do not conform any longer to the pattern of this world, but be transformed by the renewing of your mind.

ROMANS 12:2

Can you identify patterns of thinking and attitudes you hold where you need to stop conforming and start transforming?

22–28 DECEMBER

Grace

The early church saw history as a five-act play, with creation, fall and the story of Israel as the first three acts, and the drama reaching its climax in the fourth act, the events concerning Jesus of Nazareth. The early church itself was living in the fifth act, where the actors are charged with the task and responsibility of improvising the final scenes of the play on the basis of all that has gone before.

N.T. WRIGHT[32]

In his Gospel, John declares, 'Grace and truth came through Jesus Christ' (1:17). In the following readings we explore what it means to receive his outrageous grace.

✣

— 22 DECEMBER —

Forgiveness

A few days later, when Jesus again entered Capernaum, the people heard that he had come home. So many gathered that there was no room left, not even outside the door, and he preached the word to them. Some men came, bringing to him a paralytic, carried by four of them. Since they could not get him to Jesus because of the crowd, they made an opening in the roof above Jesus and, after digging through it, lowered the mat the paralysed man was lying on. When Jesus saw their faith, he said to the paralytic, 'Son, your sins are forgiven.' Now some teachers of the law were sitting there, thinking to themselves, 'Why does this fellow talk like that? He's blaspheming! Who can forgive sins but God alone?' Immediately Jesus knew in his spirit that this was what they were thinking in their hearts, and he said to them, 'Why are you thinking these things? Which is easier: to say to the paralytic, "Your sins are forgiven," or to say, "Get up, take your mat and walk"? But that you may know that the Son of Man has authority on earth to forgive sins…' He said to the paralytic, 'I tell you, get up, take your mat and go home.' He got up, took his mat and walked out in full view of them all. This amazed everyone and they praised God, saying, 'We have never seen anything like this!'

MARK 2:1–12

Desperate situations call, at times, for desperate measures. Four men heard that Jesus was in town and knew of his healing power. They decided to take a paralysed friend to meet him in the hope of a miracle. Imagine their disappointment when they saw the size of the crowd! Yet, undeterred, they climbed to the flat roof, dug a hole in the flimsy covering and lowered their bedbound friend into the centre of the action.

Jesus was impressed by the faith and devotion of the men but, instead of saying what was expected ('Be healed!'), he told the paralysed man that he forgave his sins—which was probably the last thing on the man's mind at the time.

Mark moves the drama to the next surprising scene. Some religious teachers who heard Jesus say these words were immediately offended—but kept their thoughts to themselves. Jesus opened the door wide to their private thoughts by asking a provocative question.

Their objection was a question of authority. No one has the right to offer forgiveness except God alone. 'Who does this man think he is?' was the nub of their objection, and Jesus' response was intended to demonstrate a vital point.

Everyone knew the answer to Jesus' question, 'Which is easier…?' (v. 9). Of course it was harder to make a paralysed man walk than to utter some vague words about forgiveness. So when Jesus performed the miracle and the man rose to his feet, his point was beyond further question. If he had power to mend a broken body, then his words of forgiveness—about mending a broken spirit—must carry weight too.

A respected scholar has noted that disease and sin are in some way organically connected, and so 'Jesus' healing miracles are sacraments of forgiveness'.[33]

Like the paralysed man on his mat, we are unable to help ourselves when it comes to the business of forgiveness. The grace of God, demonstrated in the death of Christ on our behalf, is our only grounds for confidence. In Jesus Christ all authority rests. His sacrificial death has made atonement for sin, once and for all, and those who come with penitent and believing hearts may know the transforming kiss of forgiveness.

Not only is the record set straight with God and with those we may have wronged, but grace enables us to begin to forgive ourselves as well.

— Reflect —

He himself bore our sins in his body on the tree, so that
we might die to sins and live for righteousness; by his wounds
you have been healed.

1 PETER 2:24

What are the implications of this statement for you?

✣

— 23 DECEMBER —

Faith

But because of his great love for us, God, who is rich in mercy, made us alive with Christ even when we were dead in transgressions—it is by grace you have been saved. And God raised us up with Christ and seated us with him in the heavenly realms in Christ Jesus, in order that in the coming ages he might show the incomparable riches of his grace, expressed in his kindness to us in Christ Jesus. For it is by grace you have been saved, through faith—and this not from yourselves, it is the gift of God—not by works, so that no one can boast. For we are God's workmanship, created in Christ Jesus to do good works, which God prepared in advance for us to do.

EPHESIANS 2:4–10

Some things stick in our minds, such as dates from school history lessons, or lines from a favourite film. I tend to remember quotes I have heard or read.

Our reading reminds us of another of the gifts that comes to us through grace—faith. I recall a sermon I heard as a new Christian. The topic was faith, and the preacher gave this definition: 'If you do before you get it, what you would do if you had it, then you've got it!' It stuck with me and helped my understanding at the time, but it missed an essential element, which is contained in today's reading.

Paul, who wrote the letter to the church in Ephesus, reminds the congregation of all the good things that are theirs in Christ. They were once dead in sin, but in his grace God made them alive through Jesus. Then Paul writes a famous and often-quoted sentence: 'For it is by grace you have been saved, through faith—and this not from yourselves, it is the gift of God—not by works, so that no one can boast' (vv. 8–9).

There is no room for human pride (boasting) as none of us can save ourselves. Church attendance, acts of charity and being kind are all good things, but none of them can make us right with God. Paul's point is that the basis of our new relationship with God is sheer grace—favour that we don't deserve. John Stott has written, 'We shall not be able to strut round heaven like peacocks. Heaven will be filled with the exploits of Christ and the praises of God.'[34]

Do you notice that faith is mentioned as the access point to God's grace? We are saved by grace, through faith. Here is the part that some people misunderstand: faith itself is a gift from God.

Imagine you are trapped in a burning building and someone comes to rescue you. They find a ladder and place it against the upstairs window and you make your way down safely, away from the flames. You are rescued through an act of kindness, and your means of accessing that kindness is the ladder provided. Grace is the basis of our rescue, and faith is the means by which we receive it for ourselves.

Here is an important discovery: we don't have to rummage around to find our own ladder. It has all been done for us in Jesus Christ. I sometimes meet people who feel they have to go away and psych themselves up to some level of spiritual fervour before they can begin to follow Jesus. I have friends who have said despairingly, 'I just haven't got the faith', and many look puzzled when I congratulate them for being at a good starting point.

Faith is for the empty-handed. John Calvin wrote, 'Faith, then, brings a man empty to God, that he may be filled with the blessings of Christ.'[35]

— Reflect —

Our reading teaches us that we are created to do good works already prepared for us by God. Spend some time praying and thinking about what they might be and write them down.

Holy Father, thank you for the gift of faith and the riches of grace. Help me to find those things that are uniquely prepared for me to do. In the name of Jesus, your Son. Amen

✣

— 24 DECEMBER —

Freedom

Some time later, Jesus went up to Jerusalem for a feast of the Jews. Now there is in Jerusalem near the Sheep Gate a pool, which in Aramaic is called Bethesda and which is surrounded by five covered colonnades. Here a great number of disabled people used to lie—the blind, the lame, the paralysed. One who was there had been an invalid for thirty-eight years. When Jesus saw him lying there and learned that he had been in this condition for a long time, he asked him, 'Do you want to get well?' 'Sir,' the invalid replied, 'I have no one to help me into the pool when the water is stirred. While I am trying to get in, someone else goes down ahead of me.' Then Jesus said to him, 'Get up! Pick up your mat and walk.' At once the man was cured; he picked up his mat and walked.

JOHN 5:1–9

Jesus' question seems, at best, tactless and, at worst, heartless. You would sympathise if the invalid replied, 'Why do you think I'm here?' But Jesus was asking a diagnostic question—one that penetrated deep into this man's conscience. His words still have that effect today (see Hebrews 4:12).

The man spent his days with a large group of disabled people at a well-known pool in Jerusalem surrounded by a covered area, which gave shade from the hot sun. The waters were said to have healing properties, and local legend claimed that when the pool was disturbed, the first sick person to immerse themselves in it would be healed. The religious authorities did not sanction this superstitious thinking but the location provided a kind of day centre for the disabled who would rely on the charitable gifts of passers-by.

The man at the centre of the story was a long-term resident, probably brought there each day by a family member and left in his usual spot. His response to Jesus' question sounds like a well-rehearsed and oft-repeated speech. It was the 'Pity me' song sung to the tune of 'It's not fair'. But Jesus had struck the heart of the issue: 'Do you really *want* to be free?'

The man had become comfortable with his sickness: it provided identity, security and a means of living. His problem defined him, gave shape to his life and probably allowed him to avoid other, uncomfortable issues such as working at a job and providing for the wider family. As a pastor, I have met a few people who seem actually to 'enjoy bad health' because it provides an escape from the harsh realities of the real world.

Notice, however, that Jesus' invitation to get up and walk was met with an eager response, an immediate acceptance, which confirmed the full effect of the miracle. The knock on the door was met with a decisive 'Yes!'

I know what it is like to hide behind a chorus of excuses and to shelter under a cloud of mediocrity rather than embrace the risk of freedom. Freedom carries implications that make demands. As this healed invalid would soon discover, a freed life needs a different shape.

A young couple went on honeymoon and, due to a flight delay, arrived at their hotel in the early hours. In the morning they complained to the manager that their room was ridiculously small, had no windows and was furnished with a single bed settee. Having booked a honeymoon suite, they'd been given a box room.

The manager accompanied them upstairs and asked if they had noticed the double doors, which the couple had assumed to be the doors of a wardrobe. He opened them to reveal a sumptuous room complete with four-poster bed, a balcony with a sea view, flowers and bottle of champagne in an ice bucket.

Mr and Mrs Glum had spent their wedding night in the lobby of the best suite in the hotel.

— Reflect —

Praise be to the God and Father of our Lord Jesus Christ,
who has blessed us in the heavenly realms with
every spiritual blessing in Christ.

EPHESIANS 1:3

Am I settling for the 'lobby' rather than entering into all that God has for me in Christ?

Where in my life do I need to experience true freedom?

✣

— 25 DECEMBER —

Family

He was in the world, and though the world was made through him, the world did not recognise him. He came to that which was his own, but his own did not receive him. Yet to all who received him, to those who believed in his name, he gave the right to become children of God—children born not of natural descent, nor of human decision or a husband's will, but born of God. The Word became flesh and made his dwelling among us. We have seen his glory, the glory of the One and Only, who came from the Father, full of grace and truth. John testifies concerning him. He cries out, saying, 'This was he of whom I said, "He who comes after me has surpassed me because he was before me."' From the fullness of his grace we have all received one blessing after another. For the law was given through Moses; grace and truth came through Jesus Christ.

JOHN 1:10–17

For many people, Christmas is a time for families to get together and celebrate, but not everyone sees it that way. Christmas can be a time when loss is felt more keenly, and when people are troubled by pain and regret. For some, life at home brings only violence and abuse.

Whatever our circumstances, God's word encourages us as we see that one gift of grace is the gift of a new family—a place where all who love Jesus belong.

John's Gospel opens with his famous 'prologue', about which reams of paper have been filled. Some experts have sought to explain it by delving into the influence of Greek philosophy, as well as the messianic expectations within first-century Judaism—but too often the study of individual trees can lead to the wood being overlooked altogether.

John was a fisherman who, together with his brother James, responded to Jesus' call to follow him. John's Gospel is an undisguised effort to persuade others to make the same choice (see John 20:31).

Our reading today, taken from part of the prologue, reminds us that Jesus went unrecognised by many and was rejected by his own people. The Creator became a creature and was crucified. Yet those who, like John, received and believed in Jesus, were given the right of adoption into the family of God. This new birth remains a supernatural gift of God but is available to all who trust in Christ.

Theologically, the picture of adoption is used elsewhere in the New Testament. Several things follow from this act of grace. First, we have a new name as apprentices (disciples) of Christ. We are more than just people who choose to go to church instead of washing the car. The word 'Christian' probably began as a nickname, as early followers were described as 'Christ ones' (see Acts 11:26).

Second, we have a new identity as we are set free from condemnation. One Ugandan evangelist was given the name 'Romans 8 verse 1' at his baptism, because he never wanted to forget who he had become in Christ. Look up the verse and you will see why it is such a wonderful spiritual birth certificate.

Third, we have a new destiny. Paul, writing about a future time when God's great salvation plan will be complete, says, 'The creation waits in eager expectation for the sons of God to be revealed' (Romans 8:19). The Greek word translated 'waits in eager expectation' means 'to wait with the head raised, and the eye fixed on that point of the horizon from which the expected object is to come'. It depicts somebody standing on tiptoe or craning forward in order to be able to see.

Creation holds its breath, anticipating all that God has in store. Do we?

— Reflect —

Almighty God, you have given us your only-begotten Son to take our nature upon him and as at this time to be born of a pure virgin: grant that we, who have been born again and made your children by adoption and grace may daily be renewed by your Holy Spirit; through Jesus Christ our Lord.

THE COLLECT FOR CHRISTMAS DAY[36]

✣

— 26 DECEMBER —

Fulfilment

Therefore Jesus said again, 'I tell you the truth, I am the gate for the sheep. All who ever came before me were thieves and robbers, but the sheep did not listen to them. I am the gate; whoever enters through me will be saved. He will come in and go out, and find pasture. The thief comes only to steal and kill and destroy; I have come that they may have life, and have it to the full. I am the good shepherd. The good shepherd lays down his life for the sheep. The hired hand is not the shepherd who owns the sheep. So when he sees the wolf coming, he abandons the sheep and runs away. Then the wolf attacks the flock and scatters it. The man runs away because he is a hired hand and cares nothing for the sheep. I am the good shepherd; I know my sheep and my sheep know me—just as the Father knows me and I know the Father—and I lay down my life for the sheep.'

JOHN 10:7–15

Today's reading contains two of the seven 'I am' statements of Jesus in John's Gospel. 'I am the gate,' he claims (v. 7), using a picture of a shepherd lying across the entrance of an open-air sheepfold to protect his vulnerable flock. By contrast, the sheep rustler kills, destroys and steals.

Developing the analogy, Jesus declares himself to be the good shepherd (v. 11), committed to the welfare of the flock, as opposed to the hired hand who saves his skin by running away when danger strikes.

Both word-pictures convey the sense of integrity and security found only in Jesus, contrasted with the 'in it for what we get out of it' attitude of the thief and hired hand. The difference is seen starkly in the statement, 'I lay down my life for the sheep' (v. 15), as these words foreshadow the brutal reality fulfilled in the crucifixion.

Another sentence in our reading introduces a further gift of grace, namely fulfilment: 'I have come that they may have life, and have it to the full' (v. 10). As the shepherd enables the sheep to feed in safety, so, in Christ, we can be and do all that God created us to be and do.

This is the very opposite of a life weighed down with religious rules and 'ought to' expectations. Rather, it is a tantalizing hint of what life in the Spirit can and should be. Paul tells one congregation that their bodies are temples of the Holy Spirit (1 Corinthians 6:19)—a thought that, according to Tom Wright, 'ought to make us shiver in our shoes'[37] (that is, shiver with holy joy rather than naked terror).

The Spirit of God within us leads us on the path of personal fulfilment as we grow in character, gifts and discipline. He enables us corporately as we grow in love and service as members of Christ's body, the Church. The Holy Spirit helps us to grow in society as we find our unique role as followers of Christ in the world.

To be honest, there are times when I wonder what happened to this life of fulfilment, because it seems to have missed me completely! But when I stop and think, I realise that it's because my focus is misplaced and my energies are misspent. With Jesus at the centre of my life, I rediscover that God-given sense of fulfilment as a bedrock to my soul. I need to heed the call to come home to him more often.

In the final seconds of the film *Patch Adams* (1998), the young medical student played by Robin Williams declares, 'All of life is a coming home. Salesmen, secretaries, coalminers, beekeepers, sword swallowers, all of us. All the restless hearts of the world, all trying to find a way home... Home. The dictionary defines it as both a place of origin and a goal or destination.'

— Reflect —

'But seek first his kingdom and his righteousness, and all these things will be given to you as well.'

MATTHEW 6:33

Take stock of your life in the light of this statement. Are changes needed to help you adjust your focus and rediscover fulfilment?

✣

— 27 DECEMBER —

Future

On his arrival, Jesus found that Lazarus had already been in the tomb for four days. Bethany was less than two miles from Jerusalem, and many Jews had come to Martha and Mary to comfort them in the loss of their brother. When Martha heard that Jesus was coming, she went out to meet him, but Mary stayed at home. 'Lord,' Martha said to Jesus, 'if you had been here, my brother would not have died. But I know that even now God will give you whatever you ask.' Jesus said to her, 'Your brother will rise again.' Martha answered, 'I know he will rise again in the resurrection at the last day.' Jesus said to her, 'I am the resurrection and the life. He who believes in me will live, even though he dies; and whoever lives and believes in me will never die. Do you believe this?' 'Yes, Lord,' she told him, 'I believe that you are the Christ, the Son of God, who was to come into the world.'

JOHN 11:17–27

Sometimes Jesus didn't act in the way people expected. That was the experience of three close friends of his—two sisters, Martha and Mary, and their brother Lazarus. Their home in Bethany had become a haven for Jesus, a getaway from the crowds that increasingly followed him around and gave him little rest.

When Lazarus first fell ill, the sisters sent for Jesus, but he chose to stay put for another two days (see v. 6). By the time he arrived, his friend had died and the funeral was over. It must have been quite a scene—a grief-stricken family, a team of comforters and a list of questions: Why the delay? Why no answer? Why no miracle? Why no explanation? Why no favour shown to friends?

Something was being painted on a larger canvas, which would commemorate this beloved family long after their own funerals. Here was the author of life staring the monster of death in the face and signalling its demise. Its tyranny was ending and the fast-approaching events of the first Easter would strip it of its power for ever. As the title of a famous book by 17th-century theologian John Owen expresses it, Easter would mean 'the death of death, in the death of Christ'.

Jesus raised Lazarus and tears were turned to laughter, but not before Martha had made her brave confession of faith—her belief that here, in her own back yard, stood the Lord of life.

We are called to be Easter people, confessing the hope that through Christ we shall be raised and shall experience what some have called 'life after life-after-death'. This is another gift of grace—our future secure in Christ.

Yesterday I received news of the death of a friend who had been a colleague for twelve years. I was relieved that her suffering had ended but desperately sad for her grieving family. Just before sitting down to type this chapter, I wrote Beth's name in my diary and added the words 'Promoted to higher service'. I think the phrase originated with the Salvation Army, and it conveys a rich theological truth: because of Christ, we have a future and a living hope.

That is why we are urged not to 'grieve like the rest of men, who have no hope' (1 Thessalonians 4:13). Grief is natural and is an expression of our love for those who have died. Jesus himself wept at Lazarus' grave, even when he knew that he was going to raise him; his tears remind us that God is not indifferent to our pain. As followers of Christ, though, we are allowed the privilege of a grief filled with the hope that the grave is not the end of the story.

How should this hope shape our vision of the future? When we experience loss, what comfort do we find in the gospel?

— Reflect: A marvellous healing —

He ran
through the unfamiliar sunlight,
drinking it in,
experiencing all at once
the thousand and one feelings
that for so long had been denied him

It was a marvellous healing:
to be so wonderfully restored,
made whole,
rebuilt.
It had just surprised him,
a little,
that he had to die
to receive it.

GERARD KELLY[38]

✣

— 28 DECEMBER —

Fruitfulness

But the fruit of the Spirit is love, joy, peace, patience, kindness, goodness, faithfulness, gentleness and self-control. Against such things there is no law. Those who belong to Christ Jesus have crucified the sinful nature with its passions and desires. Since we live by the Spirit, let us keep in step with the Spirit. Let us not become conceited, provoking and envying each other.

GALATIANS 5:22–26

The final gift of grace that we shall consider is fruitfulness. Paul wrote to several congregations reminding them of the positives and negatives of following Christ. Negatively, there were old ways of life that needed to be abandoned: Paul refers to them as 'acts of the sinful nature' and lists a few so that his readers are left in no doubt (see Galatians 5:19–21).

Positively, he writes of the fruit of God's Spirit growing in the lives of those who consistently seek to keep marching to the rhythm of his drumbeat. 'Keep in step with the Spirit' he shouts (v. 25), like a coach from the bench.

We spent several years working in France, and close to our home were acres of vineyards. I would often take a long route back from the office so that I could drive slowly through the fields of vines. I never ceased to be amazed at the contrast through the seasons. In September, around harvest, they were laden with full, ripe grapes sheltered by canopies of bright foliage; yet, by November, all that was left were rows of gnarled, naked vines. Come January, the workers would be cutting the vines down to size, and I often wondered how those wizened stumps would ever grow again.

I came to understand Jesus' teaching about the vine and the branches in a new way (see John 15:1–4), just as his disciples grasped the picture. Jesus is the vine; we are the branches. As we remain grafted into him, the life of his Spirit flows through us, making all the necessary changes in us from the old nature to the new. The Father is the gardener who prunes the branches, cutting away the dead wood and encouraging greater growth.

The fruit is a rich crop: love, joy, peace, patience, kindness, goodness, faithfulness, gentleness and self-control. As Paul points out, there is no law banning these kinds of qualities. On the contrary, any community enjoying them in large measure would become a safe and happy place to live.

Notice, though, the blunt realism in Paul's advice, reminding us that this is not candyfloss theology. He acknowledges that the old nature can raise its ugly head, with conceit, envy and the ability to wind each other up. Remember, also, that he is writing to a group of churches. The Father's gardening work is badly needed in all our lives so don't be surprised if, as you pray for the fruit of patience, you discover, through some testing situations, just how much you need it. Those are the divine pruning shears at work again.

Recently I was hurt by the behaviour of some fellow Christians and felt angry towards them. Then I realised that although I had no power to change their attitude, I was responsible for my own feelings. Their absence of fruit was no excuse to let mine go missing. Thomas à Kempis wrote in his classic book, *The Imitation of Christ*:

Gladly we desire to make other men perfect but we will not amend our own fault; we will that other men be straightly corrected and we ourselves will not be corrected. Other men's large licence displeaseth us but we to ourselves will have nothing denied that we ask. We will have others restrained by statutes and we will suffer ourselves in no wise to be more restrained. And thus it appeareth how seldom we weigh our neighbour as ourselves.[39]

— Reflect —

The fruit of the Spirit comes in nine flavours. Take a few minutes to pray over each one, asking that this coming year will be a time of personal growth.

Heavenly Father, make my heart fertile soil in which the fruit of your Spirit can grow. Cut away those things that hinder growth and make me more like Jesus in my attitudes, words and actions. Amen

29 DECEMBER—4 JANUARY

Followers

In God's story… the piece between Jesus and his work on the cross and the final chapter is still being written. God's story is not just about what God has done, but also about what God… is doing now. God is still writing the story, and, incredibly, God has invited us to participate in that writing.

BRYANT L. MYERS[40]

In the next seven readings we shall consider the implications of hearing and obeying the call of Jesus.

✣

— 29 DECEMBER —

'Come to me'

Abruptly Jesus broke into prayer: 'Thank you, Father, Lord of heaven and earth. You've concealed your ways from sophisticates and know-it-alls, but spelled them out clearly to ordinary people. Yes, Father, that's the way you like to work.' Jesus resumed talking to the people, but now tenderly. 'The Father has given me all these things to do and say. This is a unique Father–Son operation, coming out of Father and Son intimacies and knowledge. No one knows the Son the way the Father does, nor the Father the way the Son does. But I'm not keeping it to myself; I'm ready to go over it line by line with anyone willing to listen. Are you tired? Worn out? Burned out on religion? Come to me. Get away with me and you'll recover your life. I'll show you how to take a real rest. Walk with me and work with me—watch how I do it. Learn the unforced rhythms of grace. I won't lay anything heavy or ill-fitting on you. Keep company with me and you'll learn to live freely and lightly.'

MATTHEW 11:25–30 (*THE MESSAGE*)

This week we are using Eugene Peterson's paraphrase, *The Message*, offering fresh insight into familiar words.

Today we read an invitation from Jesus to weary people. This kind of weariness is not simply to do with the demands of daily life, draining though they are. Jesus is referring to the burden of religious duty, which, for many people in his day, was an unbearable load to carry (see Matthew 23:1–4).

For ordinary people trailing in the slipstream of the supersonic religious élite, life was surrounded by man-made rules and traditions, hemmed in by standards that decreed who was in and out of divine favour and haunted by the crushing sense that, no matter how hard they tried, they would never be good enough for God.

It must have been like feeling refreshing rain in a desert to hear this invitation from Jesus, who claimed an intimate relationship with God like no one else's, and called everyone to share in it also.

The more familiar translation of verse 29 starts, 'Take my yoke upon you and learn from me.' For his Jewish listeners, Jesus' words had deep resonance, as Michael Green explains:

The yoke was the wooden collar that ran across the shoulders of a pair of oxen and enabled them jointly to pull enormous weights. Metaphorically, the yoke was used to describe the law, which the Jewish youth undertook to bind to himself in the bar mitzvah ceremony. It spoke of loyal commitment. And here the carpenter of Nazareth, who had made many a yoke, says in effect, 'My yokes fit well. They do not rub your neck and shoulders. Come to me. Get yoked up to me. Make an act of loyal obedience, like a bar mitzvah, to me. And you will find a deep peace and satisfaction that you could never find elsewhere. I have come for you. Come to me.'[41]

What does it mean to 'learn the unforced rhythms of grace'? There are two lessons for us.

- First, it involves accepting that we are loved unconditionally. Outrageous grace says we can't do anything to make God love us more. The ground of our confidence is all that God has done for us in Christ: 'Because of his great love for us, God, who is rich in mercy, made us alive with Christ even when we were dead in transgressions' (Ephesians 2:4–5).
- Second, it involves living in the good of this truth, believing that the grace of God is big enough to carry us through whatever challenges we face, because it is always sufficient (see 2 Corinthians 12:9).

These are great antidotes to the feelings of inadequacy that beset all of us from time to time. We never will be adequate, but the welcome words of grace from Jesus say, 'Walk, work and watch.'

— Reflect —

Think about Jesus' invitation. Do you need to discover (or rediscover) what it means to live 'freely and lightly'? Are there things you need to lay down in order to wear his easier yoke?

✣

— 30 DECEMBER —

'Follow me'

After John was arrested, Jesus went to Galilee preaching the Message of God: 'Time's up! God's kingdom is here. Change your life and believe the Message.' Passing along the beach of Lake Galilee, he saw Simon and his brother Andrew net-fishing. Fishing was their regular work. Jesus said to them, 'Come with me. I'll make a new kind of fisherman out of you. I'll show you how to catch men and women instead of perch and bass.' They didn't ask questions. They dropped their nets and followed. A dozen yards or so down the beach, he saw the brothers James and John, Zebedee's sons. They were in the boat, mending their fishnets. Right off, he made the same offer. Immediately, they left their father Zebedee, the boat, and the hired hands, and followed.

MARK 1:14–20 (*THE MESSAGE*)

Dr George Carey, former Archbishop of Canterbury, tells the story of an officer cadet who failed at military academy. One of his instructors wrote a damning assessment: 'The only reason anyone would follow this man is out of a sense of curiosity.' He was obviously not someone who inspired confidence in those he was called to lead. We have a different picture of Jesus!

Many people have wondered about the call of those first disciples. Mark gives details of how four of the twelve began a journey that changed their lives. Two sets of brothers earned their living by fishing in Lake Galilee, which even today remains a viable business opportunity. So what made them drop everything and follow Jesus?

Anyone who has family and work responsibilities knows that you can't just leave everything and run, no matter how tempting that option may sometimes appear. I have often puzzled about what it was that gave Peter, Andrew, James and John such a sudden rush of blood to the head that they promptly dropped their nets.

The conclusion I have reached is that Jesus knew these men already, and there had been some kind of build-up to the incident on the lake shore. Perhaps he had taken them into his confidence by explaining some of what God had called him to do. Maybe they had had time to make arrangements for their wider families to be looked after while they were away. It's an argument from silence, I know, but it is utterly consistent with a God who cares about the details of life (see Matthew 6:25–34).

Whether or not my theory is correct, the lakeside encounter signals a 'now' moment. As if they were paratroopers lined up at the jump hatch, the green light for 'Go' signals action.

Do you notice the analogy that Jesus uses in his invitation? He tells the men of a new kind of fishing: they will be out to catch people instead of fish. This promise came true, as these four fishermen were among the first witnesses who spread the message of God's rescue plan for lost people. In Peter's case, over 3000 would be caught up into faith as a result of his astonishing sermon on the Day of Pentecost (see Acts 2:14–41).

When we answer Christ's call to follow, we have little idea of where it will lead, but we can take heart from the stories of those who, having obeyed, found surprise, opportunity, joy and fulfilment. These fishermen offer a stirring example of what robust apprenticeship looks like. Jesus called and they answered with an unhesitating faith.

Whether we are seasoned travellers or new to the journey (or perhaps thinking seriously about starting out), it is important to recall that we are not alone. Jesus himself has promised to travel with us all the way (Matthew 28:20).

— Reflect —

Donald Miller points out in his bestselling book, *Blue Like Jazz*, that discipleship is a journey in which, as we travel toward God's future, he walks towards us:

'I am early in my story, but I believe I will stretch out into eternity and in heaven I will reflect upon these earlier days, these days when it seems God was down a dirt road, walking towards me. Years ago he was a singing speck in the distance, now He is close enough I can hear his singing. Soon I will see the lines on His face.'[42]

✣

— 31 DECEMBER —

'Wait for me'

Dear Theophilus, in the first volume of this book I wrote on everything that Jesus began to do and teach until the day he said goodbye to the apostles, the ones he had chosen through the Holy Spirit, and was taken up to heaven. After his death, he presented himself alive to them in many different settings over a period of forty days. In face-to-face meetings, he talked to them about things concerning the kingdom of God. As they met and ate meals together, he told them that they were on no account to leave Jerusalem but 'must wait for what the Father promised: the promise you heard from me. John baptised in water; you will be baptised in the Holy Spirit. And soon.' When they were together for the last time they asked, 'Master, are you going to restore the kingdom to Israel now? Is this the time?' He told them, 'You don't get to know the time. Timing is the Father's business. What you'll get is the Holy Spirit. And when the Holy Spirit comes on you, you will be able to be my witnesses in Jerusalem, all over Judea and Samaria, even to the ends of the world.' These were his last words. As they watched, he was taken up and disappeared in a cloud.

ACTS 1:1–9 (*THE MESSAGE*)

Today is a doorway between the year that is past and the new year to come, and we are reminded that to follow Christ we need his Spirit within us.

Our reading takes us to a 40-day period during which the resurrected Jesus met with his followers and taught about the kingdom of God. One vital piece of information was that they were to stay in Jerusalem and wait for the promised gift of the Holy Spirit.

This must have been a tough instruction to follow. Shortly Jesus would return to heaven, leaving his followers in the very city where, a few weeks earlier, they had seen their Lord nailed to a cross. The men behind that act of injustice still held the levers of power. Besides, many of the followers were from 'up north' in the region of Galilee and consequently had little reason to stay in Jerusalem. But Jesus told them to wait, so that is what they did.

Waiting is never easy, especially when we feel that it's a pointless exercise, but waiting seems to be a spiritual discipline that God wants his children to learn, as the stories of Abraham, Simeon, Anna and others reveal.

From our standpoint, we can see the sense behind Jesus' insistence that they should wait in Jerusalem. The Day of Pentecost was not far off, and a remarkable transformation would take place on that day in these cautious followers (see Acts 2:1–42). Peter would preach powerfully, 3000 people would be baptised as new followers and the community of Christ's people would never be the same again. It would be the start of what Jesus had promised: the gift of the Holy Spirit would enable his people to take the gospel to the whole world.

On this eve of a new year, we are reminded of two things. First, God delights to give the Holy Spirit freely to his children (see Luke 11:11–13) and, second, this gift is indispensable if we are to live in the strength of Christ's power (see Ephesians 1:17–21).

The waiting for Pentecost is over, Christ has ascended to heaven and his Spirit has been poured out. Let us ask God for a new filling of the Holy Spirit, allowing him access to every room of our lives, especially those that remain locked and in urgent need of a spring-clean.

— Reflect —

God and Father of our Lord Jesus Christ, whose years never fail and whose mercies are new each returning day: let the radiance of your Spirit renew our lives, warming our hearts and giving light to our minds; that we may pass the coming year in joyful obedience and firm faith; through him who is the beginning and the end, your Son Christ our Lord. Amen

COLLECT FOR NEW YEAR'S EVE[43]

✣

— 1 JANUARY —

'Go for me'

Meanwhile, the eleven disciples were on their way to Galilee, headed for the mountain Jesus had set for their reunion. The moment they saw him they worshipped him. Some, though, held back, not sure about worship, about risking themselves totally. Jesus, undeterred, went right ahead and gave his charge: 'God authorised and commanded me to commission you: Go out and train everyone you meet, far and near, in this way of life, marking them by baptism in the threefold name: Father, Son, and Holy Spirit. Then instruct them in the practice of all I have commanded you. I'll be with you as you do this, day after day after day, right up to the end of the age.'

MATTHEW 28:16–20 (*THE MESSAGE*)

Matthew closes his Gospel with Jesus' final charge to his followers—not just the ten standing with Matthew on the mountain that day but all who would become fellow apprentices in the future.

We are followers with a clear set of instructions: having found faith in Christ, we are to pass it on. These words of Jesus are often called the Great Commission but it has been pointed out that they could be more accurately described as the Great Omission—the command that we are most likely to overlook.

Our reading spells out what the commission means: it involves training and instructing people to become followers of Christ in a manner that is sealed by baptism and fleshed out in obedient discipleship. Notice the four words that make all the difference: 'I'll be with you' (v. 20). We are not on our own in the task. The presence of the risen Jesus is with us in the person of the Holy Spirit.

Many of us find it embarrassing to talk about our faith, perhaps lacking the confidence to answer difficult questions. Some of us admit to being fearful of ridicule or rejection. We are not alone in such insecurities.

Francis Schaeffer was an influential thinker and writer, described as one of the most important figures in 20th-century Christianity. He struggled throughout his life with the feeling that he had to convince people about the Christian gospel and, if they didn't accept it, he had failed in some way. His close friend Hans Rookmaaker records a lesson that Schaeffer constantly relearned:

If God calls us to speak to somebody we try to give the best possible answers, but at the same time we pray that God will work in that person's heart so that whatever we say right will make itself felt and continue to work, and whatever we say wrong will have no impact. We acknowledge that it is first of all God's work rather than our work. Then the pressure is gone and because of that it is not so exhausting.[44]

This is a vitally important lesson to learn. It's not our job to bring people to faith—this is God's work—but we are called to assist in whatever way we can through being available to offer friendship, to pray faithfully for those who struggle with deep questions, to show practical care and to 'always be prepared to give an answer to everyone who asks you to give the reason for the hope that you have' (1 Peter 3:15).

Think of the role of a midwife or doctor assisting with a birth, which is a thoroughly natural process. Their task is to help that process through and offer whatever skill and support they can, so the baby may be born safely and offered first-class care in those first minutes of life. This is a helpful picture of our role as individuals and local congregations, standing ready to help in the Spirit-directed process of people coming to faith in Christ.

The words of Jesus' commission remind us that church is not an exclusive holy club, open to a few. As Archbishop William Temple remarked, it is the only organization that exists for the benefit of non-members. May we play our part this year in building church without walls.

— Reflect —

Think of several friends who do not yet know Christ and pray that this will be a year of discovery for them.

✣

— 2 JANUARY —

'Trust in me'

John's disciples reported back to him the news of all these events taking place. He sent two of them to the Master to ask the question, 'Are you the One we've been expecting, or are we still waiting?' The men showed up before Jesus and said, 'John the Baptiser sent us to ask you, "Are you the One we've been expecting, or are we still waiting?"' In the next two or three hours Jesus healed many from diseases, distress, and evil spirits. To many of the blind he gave the gift of sight. Then he gave his answer: 'Go back and tell John what you have just seen and heard: the blind see, the lame walk, lepers are cleansed, the deaf hear, the dead are raised, the wretched of the earth have God's salvation hospitality extended to them.'

LUKE 7:18–22 (*THE MESSAGE*)

It's not difficult to trust God when all is going well, but to keep trusting when heaven seems to have lost your file takes special grace.

John the Baptist had been given a huge task—to prepare the way of the Lord and announce his arrival (see John 1:29–34)—but his fiery preaching won him enemies in high places. King Herod was stung by John's prophetic criticism of his decision to marry his sister-in-law, and had him thrown into jail (see Matthew 14:1–4).

With time on his hands, John began to worry that he had made a mistake. He had told the crowds that the one coming after him would baptise not with water but with fire, yet the reports he received in prison didn't seem to fit what he had expected Jesus to be doing. At a deeper, more personal level, John (a man used to wide open spaces) keenly felt the pain of confinement. Jesus was not delivering in the way John had hoped. As one writer expresses it, 'John was familiar with the prophecy that the Messiah would preach deliverance to the captives, but he had not come to him. He would heal the broken hearted, but he sent no message to heal his breaking heart. Even a man of granite can be the prey of torturing doubt.'[45]

It is important to notice that Jesus didn't send an immediate reply back with John's messengers. First he let them see some of the miracles that were happening. He told them to give an eyewitness account of what they saw so that John would know there was no mistake: the poor were receiving good news, just as Isaiah had prophesied (see Isaiah 61:1–3).

Jesus then added a message that pronounced a special blessing to John as he wrestled with his doubts: 'Blessed is the man who does not fall away on account of me' (v. 23). There was no trace of condemnation in Jesus' words—quite the opposite. Luke records Jesus' public affirmation of his cousin's strong faith (see vv. 24–28). There is no shame in asking questions; it is wilful unbelief that the Bible condemns, not honest doubt.

John's 'dark night of the soul' stands as an encouragement to us when we find it hard to work out what God is up to. Jesus encouraged him to trust, even when things were not going the way John expected. Perhaps you can identify with John's dilemma at present, or look back on a period when you shared his feelings of doubt. The most honest prayer for such times is simply, 'Father, I don't understand but I do trust you.'

The blessing that Jesus promised to John extends to all who keep on keeping on when the going is tough. Draw strength from this reassurance and recognise that even people with strong faith experience times of doubt.

John's friends told him stories of miracles. We build our own faith when we hear what God is doing and trust that, before long, it may be our turn to experience it.

— Reflect —

'There is beauty in the dark valleys of life. It is called hope.'

JOAN CHITTISTER[46]

In your prayers, ask Jesus Christ for the gift of hope in those areas where you find it hard to trust.

✣

— 3 JANUARY —

'Learn from me'

'These words I speak to you are not incidental additions to your life, homeowner improvements to your standard of living. They are foundational words, words to build a life on. If you work these words into your life, you are like a smart carpenter who built his house on solid rock. Rain poured down, the river flooded, a tornado hit—but nothing moved that house. It was fixed to the rock. But if you just use my words in Bible studies and don't work them into your life, you are like a stupid carpenter who built his house on the sandy beach. When a storm rolled in and the waves came up, it collapsed like a house of cards.' When Jesus concluded his address, the crowd burst into applause. They had never heard teaching like this. It was apparent that he was living everything he was saying—quite a contrast to their religion teachers! This was the best teaching they had ever heard.

MATTHEW 7:24–29 (*THE MESSAGE*)

Every Sunday, services of Christian worship are held across the world in a rich variety of venues and surroundings. From cathedrals to cinemas, in city centres and villages, scripture will be read and sermons preached. All together, they will add up to billions of words, but their lasting impact will be determined by the type of soil into which the seed of God's word falls (see Luke 8:4–15).

I recall walking out of a country churchyard and seeing a carved inscription on the lintel of the lych-gate, 'Blessed is he who hears my words and puts them into practice.' Those words are based on today's reading—the parable of the wise and foolish builders.

This story comes at the end of the 'Sermon on the Mount', a

manifesto of the kingdom of God from the lips of Jesus himself. Like all parables, though, it makes an important point of eternal value. Jesus' words are not to be admired or simply read and remembered but are to be assimilated and applied as foundations for living.

Every follower needs to put into practice what Jesus teaches. The paraphrase of *The Message* offers a helpful picture: the teachings of Jesus are not to be seen as a home improvement, such as an extension to the house, but as a foundation on which a whole new home can be built.

Jesus paints a contrast between a wise carpenter who chose his foundation with skill and care and a foolish one who simply wanted to get the job done quickly. When the elements did what elements do, it wasn't long before the value of a good foundation was proven.

The song about the wise man building his house on a rock is among my earliest memories, but just knowing the chorus after 50-something years is not enough. Working the words of Jesus into our lives is the hallmark of a consistent follower.

In his insightful book on Jesus as a leader, Andrew Watson has a chapter entitled 'Walking the way of costly grace', based partly on a famous book by a German Christian leader, Dietrich Bonhoeffer, who taught about the importance of costly grace over and against the dangers of cheap grace. Bonhoeffer wrote:

Cheap grace is the preaching of forgiveness without requiring repentance, baptism without church discipline, communion without confession... cheap grace is grace without discipleship, grace without the cross, grace without Jesus Christ, living and incarnate. This cheap grace has been... disastrous to our own spiritual lives. Instead of opening up the way to Christ it has closed it. Instead of calling us to follow Christ, it has hardened us in our disobedience.[47]

Cheap grace comes from building on wrong foundations. The next time you attend church, spend time before the service asking God to speak to you, and then take time before you leave to pray for the ability to work his words into your life in the coming week.

— Reflect —

Trust and obey, for there's no other way
To be happy in Jesus, than to trust and obey.

JOHN HENRY SAMMIS (1846–1919)[48]

Do you struggle to be an obedient follower of Christ?

✣

— 4 JANUARY —

'Die for me'

Then he told them what they could expect for themselves: 'Anyone who intends to come with me has to let me lead. You're not in the driver's seat—I am. Don't run from suffering; embrace it. Follow me and I'll show you how. Self-help is no help at all. Self-sacrifice is the way, my way, to finding yourself, your true self. What good would it do to get everything you want and lose you, the real you? If any of you is embarrassed with me and the way I'm leading you, know that the Son of Man will be far more embarrassed with you when he arrives in all his splendour in company with the Father and the holy angels. This isn't, you realise, pie in the sky by and by. Some who have taken their stand right here are going to see it happen, see with their own eyes the kingdom of God.'

LUKE 9:23–27 (*THE MESSAGE*)

This past week we have looked at some Bible passages that spell out what following Christ entails. Our last study considers Jesus' statement, 'If anyone would come after me, he must deny himself and take up his cross daily and follow me' (v. 23, NIV). The parallel Gospel accounts omit the word 'daily', but Luke ensures that we don't lose the earthy implications of following Christ. There is more to it than just giving up an hour on a Sunday.

Bishop Tom Wright explains how central this daily cross-carrying is to the teaching of Jesus: 'At the heart of Jesus' subversive agenda was the call to his followers to take up the cross and follow him, to become his companions in the alternative kingdom-story he was enacting.'[49]

When Jesus chose this word-picture, it would have sent a shudder down the spines of his first listeners. This was not a text for a stained-glass window but a gruesome reminder of the power of the Roman empire and the brutal treatment given to any who chose to challenge that power.[50] It was common to see prisoners carrying a beam of wood to which they would be nailed and left to die naked, hanging in the sun by a roadside. In marketing terms, Jesus could not have thought of a more negative image with which to invite people to embrace his teaching.

The Message paraphrase gives insight to the meaning behind Jesus' call. Following Jesus means just that—following in his footsteps of total obedience to the Father, wherever that may lead and whatever it may entail. The cross-carrier has lost his or her rights. True disciples move out of the driving seat.

When I was at theological college, a noticeboard displayed a text from one of Paul's letters: 'Therefore, I urge you, brothers, in view of God's mercy, to offer your bodies as living sacrifices, holy and pleasing to God—this is your spiritual act of worship' (Romans 12:1). An anonymous student wrote underneath in felt-tip, 'The trouble with a living sacrifice is, it keeps crawling off the altar!'

The desire to do our own thing is not far from any of us. I have no problem with the concept of serving others, until people start treating me like a servant! Pride and arrogant independence are just two characteristics, among others, that need facing down daily.

The call of Jesus is a call to die to self-interest, self-satisfaction and self-centredness. Jim Elliott was a young missionary who was murdered by the people he was seeking to help. In his journal he wrote some reflections on Jesus' invitation for us to take up our cross. His words are profound: 'He is no fool who gives what he cannot keep to gain what he cannot lose.'[51]

— Reflect —

'If as [Jesus] himself said, following him involves taking up the cross, we should expect as the New Testament tells us repeatedly, that to build on his foundation will be to find the cross etched into the pattern of our life and work over and over again.'

BISHOP TOM WRIGHT[52]

Can you spot places where the cross is being etched into your life?

5–6 JANUARY

Future

Baptism and Eucharist are mini-dramas of salvation using material props—water, bread and wine (in some traditions, juice). By washing a new believer, and by eating and drinking together, Christians use their bodies to re-enact the story of God's gracious salvation in Christ. Through seeing, moving, touching, tasting and smelling, God speaks again the creative and redeeming Word.

DONALD MCCULLOUGH[53]

Our concluding readings remind us that the people of God have a future and a hope.

✣

— 5 JANUARY —

'Until'

When you come together, it is not the Lord's Supper you eat, for as you eat, each of you goes ahead without waiting for anybody else. One remains hungry, another gets drunk. Don't you have homes to eat and drink in? Or do you despise the church of God and humiliate those who have nothing? What shall I say to you? Shall I praise you for this? Certainly not! For I received from the Lord what I also passed on to you: the Lord Jesus, on the night he was betrayed, took bread, and when he had given thanks, he broke it and said, 'This is my body, which is for you; do this in remembrance of me.' In the same way, after supper he took the cup, saying, 'This cup is the new covenant in my blood; do this, whenever you drink it, in remembrance of me.' For whenever you eat this bread and drink this cup, you proclaim the Lord's death until he comes.

1 CORINTHIANS 11:20–26

The congregation in Corinth was in a mess. Paul, who had planted the church, pulls no punches and his blunt assessment reveals some ugly divisions in the congregation that made a mockery of the Lord's Supper or Communion service. The word 'communion' suggests partnership and sharing—but that was the opposite of what was happening.

The first Christian congregations often celebrated Holy Communion in the context of a meal, sometimes called a love feast. For many of them, it would be the best meal of the week, as food was shared freely, which was a special blessing to those who were poor.

Sadly, in Corinth this special meal divided rather than united the congregation, with the haves and the have-nots sticking out like sore thumbs. Some over-indulged to the point of getting drunk while others (possibly slaves) left the table unfed—a situation that Paul viewed as scandalous. He restates the meaning behind the meal in an attempt to get the congregation back on track.

First, he reminds them that Jesus initiated it at the Passover meal on the night of his arrest. It was not something dreamt up by church leaders but was laid down by Jesus himself. Second, Jesus told his followers that they were to take bread and wine and remember him. Later, they understood more fully the significance of his words about his body and blood being given for them. Third, Paul reminds the Corinthians that the very act of taking bread and wine proclaims the truth about Christ's redeeming death and resurrection. It retells the story of outrageous grace not only to those sharing in the act as followers, but also to onlookers, including the watching world and the principalities and powers in the heavenly realms (see Ephesians 6:12).

Finally, Paul reminds the congregation that this meal anticipates the future. We celebrate it 'until he comes' (v. 26). 'Until' is a waiting word: it promises more to come. When we take bread and wine, we do not simply look back to all that Jesus has done through the cross, but we also look forward to the final reel of the film, when that work will be completed. In the service of Holy Communion, God's future arrives into our present. We declare with confidence, 'Christ has died, Christ is risen, Christ shall come again!'

The Corinthian church needed to remember that this meal with a meaning was too important to be trivialised or abused. Do we need this reminder, too? They had lost sight of its significance. Is that true of us? They had ignored the needs of others in the family of faith. Are we similarly thoughtless? They had forgotten what the meal declared about Christian hope. Can we spot the same fault in ourselves?

— Reflect —

When God's people meet to remember and celebrate the death and resurrection of Jesus Christ in bread and wine, 'it is the breaking in of God's future, the Advent future, into our present time. Every Eucharist is a little Christmas as well as a little Easter' (Bishop Tom Wright).[54]

How can we avoid getting in a rut when we celebrate Holy Communion?

✣

— 6 JANUARY —

'Done'

Then I saw a new heaven and a new earth, for the first heaven and the first earth had passed away, and there was no longer any sea. I saw the Holy City, the new Jerusalem, coming down out of heaven from God, prepared as a bride beautifully dressed for her husband. And I heard a loud voice from the throne saying, 'Now the dwelling of God is with men, and he will live with them. They will be his people, and God himself will be with them and be their God. He will wipe every tear from their eyes. There will be no more death or mourning or crying or pain, for the old order of things has passed away.' He who was seated on the throne said, 'I am making everything new!' Then he said, 'Write this down, for these words are trustworthy and true.' He said to me: 'It is done. I am the Alpha and the Omega, the Beginning and the End. To him who is thirsty I will give to drink without cost from the spring of the water of life.'

REVELATION 21:1–6

When I was a boy, I found it hard to get enthusiastic about the idea of heaven. I felt uncomfortable growing up in a family and a church setting where everyone seemed to think it was a prospect worth talking and singing about with great enthusiasm. The problem was, my wires were crossed—badly.

I thought of an eternity of hymn singing with no time off for football or climbing trees. I attended a school where, every Thursday morning, we had a compulsory hour of hymn practice led by the indomitable Mrs King, who could have terrorised lions to behave like pussycats. If that was what heaven would be like, I was seriously worried about putting my name down.

By God's kindness, I have come to understand that the idea of disembodied souls floating on clouds, playing harps and being goaded by an angelic equivalent of Mrs King to 'sing louder!' is more a product of our culture and imagination than biblical truth.[55] In reality, it is not so much a case of us going to heaven as heaven coming to us.

The future that God has planned is what the whole world is waiting for (see Romans 8:18–21). John, in the book of Revelation, paints a picture of God bringing his great rescue plan to an astonishing fulfilment.

The imagery and language create a picture of a renewed heaven and earth worth waiting for. A beautifully dressed bride conveys ideas of joy, celebration and consummation, while the concept of God dwelling among his people suggests an end to all those things that mar our human experience. Death, tears, grief, suffering and pain are all gone for good in this new order. Then comes the emphatic, authority-laden statement, 'It is done. I am the Alpha and Omega, the Beginning and the End' (v. 6). God has the last word.

Of course we are filled with questions, like curious children, but we are looking at a poor reflection (1 Corinthians 13:12). It won't always be like that, and we have been told enough to get us excited.

We are called to be people of hope. We are not on a journey with no destination; nor are we caught in a story without an ending. We are people with a purpose, who live trusting that when God makes a promise, he delivers.

Through this book we have been reminded of God's track record as someone who speaks, acts and can be trusted wholeheartedly. Just as Abraham and Sarah, Joseph and Mary, Simeon and Anna were called to trust and follow, we are called to walk by faith rather than sight (2 Corinthians 5:7).

— Reflect —

This verse of an ancient hymn (dating back to the twelfth century) reminds us that, for generations, followers of Christ have anticipated God's future for his people—the new Jerusalem—with eager anticipation and excited joy.

Jerusalem the golden, with milk and honey blest,
Beneath thy contemplation sink heart and voice oppressed.
I know not, O I know not, what joys await us there,
What radiancy of glory, what bliss beyond compare.

BERNARD OF MORLAIX[56]

Read today's Bible passage again and reflect on the promises that God makes about the future.

✣

Postscript

We ride with our backs to the engine. We have no notion what stage in the journey we have reached... a story is precisely the sort of thing that cannot be understood until you have heard the whole of it.

C.S. LEWIS[57]

A group of soldiers were engaged in a battle on French soil during World War II. In a furious exchange of fire, one man was shot and killed. When the fighting died down, his companions took his body to a local church and asked the priest if their friend could be buried in the cemetery.

The priest enquired if the dead soldier was a baptised Roman Catholic. His friends replied that he was not, as he had been brought up a Methodist. The priest offered his condolences but said the rules clearly stated that only Catholics could be buried in the churchyard. As a gesture of kindness, though, he pointed to a field next to the cemetery and said, 'That field belongs to the church. Please bury your friend there by the fence that marks the end of the graveyard. I am sorry, but he must be buried on the other side.'

Years later, two of the soldiers made an emotional return to the church and searched for their friend's grave—but they couldn't find it. They remembered digging the grave by the fence at the edge of the cemetery as instructed. The fence was still there but there was no sign of the grave and small wooden cross that they had erected.

They went across to the church and found that the same priest was still there, although he was now an old man. They asked about their friend's grave and listened intently as the elderly priest related his story. 'That night after you left, I could not sleep,' he told them. 'My conscience was troubled and in the early hours I made an important decision. Then, first thing in the morning, I went out to the graveyard and moved the fence. You will find your friend's grave there inside our cemetery.'

As we celebrate God's gift of his Son, Jesus, it is worth recalling why 'the Word became flesh and made his dwelling among us' (John 1:14). He came to be the Saviour of the world.

He didn't come to be the Saviour for one religious type, one ethnic group or one social class. Jesus didn't bother with the barriers we often build but went out of his way to make outsiders insiders. He is the Redeemer of all who accept him.

When Jesus came, God didn't just move the fence—he took it away completely.

Truly, this is outrageous grace.

✣

Study guide

This book has been written primarily for an individual reader following each reading on a daily basis through Advent, but it can also be used in a small group where the members have followed the daily readings and reflections. The questions below are based on each week's readings and are designed to prompt thoughtful discussion and prayer.

1–7 December: Legacy

1. Abraham is described as 'the Christopher Columbus of faith'. In what ways is this a true comparison? What can we learn from his example?
2. There are a number of references to laughter and joy in these readings. Can you think of appropriate ways of more openly demonstrating this aspect of our faith?
3. As you review this week's readings on the nature of faith, what aspects challenge you most? Where do you need to grow in faith?
4. We have inherited a legacy through God's outrageous grace. What are the implications?

— Prayer —

Heavenly Father, as you spoke to Abraham and fulfilled your promises to him, speak to us afresh during this season of Advent and create in us believing hearts. In the name of Jesus, your Son and our Saviour. Amen

8–14 December: Promise

1. 'Too often we are hemmed in by the predictable and obvious, forgetting that God repeatedly chooses to use unlikely people, works in less obvious ways and shows up in unusual places' (from the reading for 8 December). Can you think of some examples that support this statement?
2. What have this week's readings shown you about the Lord Jesus Christ and his purpose in coming into the world?
3. The value of rooting ourselves in scripture has been highlighted this week (see 10 December). Identify some examples of how this might shape your prayers at the moment.
4. Read Isaiah 42:1–7 again. How does the image of Jesus as someone who will not break a bruised reed or snuff out a smouldering wick help to shape our approach to pastoral care?

— Prayer —

Father in heaven, we praise you for your faithfulness in fulfilling your promises in the past. Strengthen our faith, that we may trust your promises for today and the coming days. In Christ's name. Amen

15–21 December: Encounter

1. Which of the encounter stories made the greatest impression on you? Why?
2. Compare the responses of Zechariah and Mary to the angelic messages they received (see Luke 1:26–38, 57–66). What lessons can we draw from their contrasting reactions?
3. Joseph is described as a 'hidden hero'. Do you agree? Can you identify other hidden heroes known to you? What makes them stand out?

4. 'How sad that in many churches this element of surprise is almost entirely absent, and boring predictability governs all that happens!' (Michael Green: see 19 December). Do you agree with this comment? How can we nurture an attitude of faith and expectancy that opens the door wide to divine encounter?

— Prayer —

Lord Jesus Christ, may we encounter you in new ways and understand more fully your purpose and plan for our lives. May your Holy Spirit reveal your truth and glory. In the power of your name. Amen

22–28 December: Grace

1. This week we have considered some of the gifts of grace:
    - Forgiveness
    - Faith
    - Freedom
    - Family
    - Fulfilment
    - Future
    - Fruitfulness
2. Which of these have you seen with fresh understanding?
3. The story of the honeymoon couple (see 24 December) posed an important question: 'Am I settling for the "lobby" rather than entering into all that God has for me in Christ?' What is your response?
4. How would you explain what it means to be a member of God's family, and the blessings it brings? (See 25 December.)
5. Most readers can identify with the puzzlement of Martha and Mary at Jesus' slow response (see John 11:17–27). How should we react when Jesus doesn't act in the way we expect?

— Prayer —

Father, thank you for all that you have lavished on us in Christ. May we receive your gifts of grace with love and gratitude and give our lives to you in sacrificial service. Through Jesus Christ our Lord. Amen

29 December–4 January: Followers

1. 'God is still writing his story, and, incredibly, God has invited us to participate in that writing' (Bryant L. Myers). What have you learned this week about sharing in this great writing project?
2. As we have considered seven invitations of Jesus, which speaks most directly to you in your current situation?
3. 'Go for me...' (see 1 January). Do you find it difficult to talk about your faith? If so, why? If not, are there any tips you can offer to others?
4. 'It's not difficult to trust God when all is going well, but to keep trusting when heaven seems to have lost your file takes special grace' (see 2 January). What can we learn from John the Baptist about following in the dark?

— Prayer —

Lord Jesus Christ, we hear your call to 'follow me!' Grant us grace, courage and single-mindedness, that we may follow you closely all the days of our lives. In your name we pray. Amen

5–6 January: Future

1. Can you summarise, in your own words, the shape of Christian hope?

2. How should we prepare ourselves to celebrate Holy Communion? (See 5 January.)
3. List some of the things you have learned through this Advent and Christmas season.

— Prayer —

Heavenly Father, we thank you for your love for the world seen in your great story of salvation. Lord Jesus Christ, we praise you that you humbled yourself and became obedient to death on the cross. Holy Spirit, we glorify you that you take the things of Christ and make them real to us. Father, Son and Spirit, we embrace the future you have planned and ask that we may play our small part in your great story. Amen

Notes

1 The technical term is 'rapid dominance', and the strategy was developed by Harlan K. Ullman and James P. Wade. It is based on 'the use of overwhelming decisive force, dominant battlefield awareness, dominant manoeuvres and spectacular displays of power to paralyze an adversary's perception of the battlefield and destroy its will to fight' (*Shock and Awe: Achieving Rapid Dominance*, accessed via www.gutenberg.org/etext/7259).
2 See the final verse of 'When I survey the wondrous cross'.
3 Rob Lacey, *Are We Getting Through? A Resource Book for Creative Communication* (Silver Fish, 1999), p. 171. Email info@laceytheatrecompany.com.
4 Rowan Williams, *Open to Judgement: Sermons and Addresses* (DLT, 1994).
5 Graham Tomlin, *The Provocative Church* (SPCK, 2000), p. 26.
6 Jonathan Aitken, *Pride and Perjury* (HarperCollins, 2000).
7 Colin Sinclair, *The Hitch-Hiker's Guide to the Bible* (Monarch Books, 2008), p. 19.
8 Notice the change of name from Abram to Abraham and Sarai to Sarah: see Genesis 17:3–15 for the explanation.
9 From 'O love that wilt not let me go' by George Matheson (1842–1906).
10 C.S. Lewis, *Letters to Malcolm: Chiefly on Prayer* (Geoffrey Bles, 1964).
11 John Ortberg, *The Life You've Always Wanted* (Zondervan, 1997).
12 See, for example, how on one occasion he was driven by fear rather than faith (Genesis 12:10–20) and how he tried to fulfil God's promise of a son in his own way (Genesis 16:1–4).
13 David Pawson, *Unlocking the Bible Omnibus* (HarperCollins, 2003), p. 95.
14 John R.W. Stott, *The Message of Romans* (The Bible Speaks Today series) (IVP, 1994), p. 137.

15 Joseph Cardinal Ratzinger (now Pope Benedict XVI), *Images of Hope: Meditations on Major Feasts* (Ignatius Press, 1997).
16 Paul uses a wordplay in this letter. The name Onesimus means 'useful'. Paul is saying, 'Named useful, he proved to be useless, but now in Christ he really is useful!'
17 Lesslie Newbigin, *The Gospel in a Pluralistic Society* (SPCK, 1989), p. 227.
18 Gerard Kelly, *Spoken Worship* (Zondervan, 2007).
19 Tom Wright, *Acts for Everyone, Part 1* (SPCK, 2008) p. 72.
20 Raymond Brown, *The Message of Hebrews* (The Bible Speaks Today series) (IVP, 1982) p. 149.
21 Cited by Robert Louis Wilken (ed. trans.), *Isaiah: Interpreted by Early Christian and Medieval Commentators* (Eerdmans, 2007), p. 416.
22 William Barclay, *Daily Study Bible (Matthew's Gospel Vol. 1)* (St Andrews Press, 1956), p. 92.
23 Donald Miller, *Searching for God Knows What* (Thomas Nelson, 2004), p. 15.
24 Christopher J.H. Wright, *The Mission of God: Unlocking the Bible's Grand Narrative* (IVP, 2006), p. 533
25 R.S. Thomas, *Selected Poems* (J.M. Dent, 1996).
26 Joachim Jeremias, *Jerusalem in the Time of Jesus* (Fortress, 1975), p. 375.
27 Donald Kraybill, *The Upside Down Kingdom* (Herald Press, 1990), p. 221.
28 Jonathan Sacks, *From Optimism to Hope: Thoughts for the Day* (Continuum International, 2004).
29 J.C. Ryle (1816–1900), first Anglican Bishop of Liverpool.
30 Michael Green, *The Message of Matthew* (The Bible Speaks Today series) (IVP, 2000), p. 66.
31 Luke notes five songs in his opening two chapters: 1) Elizabeth's song, 1:42–45; 2) Mary's song, vv. 46–55; 3) Zechariah's song, vv. 68–79; 4) the angels' song, 2:14; 5) Simeon's song, vv. 29–32.

32 N.T. Wright, 'Jerusalem in the New Testament', in P.W.L. Walker (ed.), *Jerusalem Past and Present in the Purposes of God* (Paternoster/Baker, 2nd edition, 1994), p. 70.
33 C.E.B. Cranfield, cited in Donald English, *The Message of Mark* (The Bible Speaks Today series) (IVP, 1992), p. 66.
34 John Stott, *The Message of Ephesians* (The Bible Speaks Today series) (IVP, 1979), p. 83.
35 John Calvin, *Commentaries on the Epistles of Paul to the Galatians and Ephesians* (Baker Book House, 1981), p. 227.
36 *Celebrating Common Prayer: A Version of the Daily Office SSF* (Mowbray, 1992), p. 350.
37 N.T. Wright, *Simply Christian* (SPCK, 2006), p. 131.
38 Kelly, *Spoken Worship*.
39 Thomas à Kempis (1379–1471), *The Imitation of Christ* (Everyman's Library Edition) (J.M. Dent, 1910), pp. 27–28.
40 Bryant L. Myers, *Walking with the Poor: Principles and Practice of Transformational Development* (Orbis Books/World Vision, 2002), p. 23.
41 Michael Green, *The Message of Matthew* (IVP, 2000), p. 143.
42 Donald Miller, *Blue Like Jazz: Non Religious Thoughts on Christian Spirituality* (Nelson, 2003).
43 *Celebrating Common Prayer*, p. 355.
44 Colin Duriez, *Francis Schaeffer: An Authentic Life* (IVP, 2008), pp. 45–46.
45 J. Oswald Saunders, *Men from God's School* (Marshall Morgan and Scott, 1965), p. 184.
46 Joan D. Chittister, *Scarred by Struggle, Transformed by Hope* (Eerdmans, 2005).
47 Dietrich Bonhoeffer, *The Cost of Discipleship* (SCM, 14th impression 1986), quoted in Andrew Watson, *The Fourfold Leadership of Jesus* (BRF, 2008), p. 89.
48 From the hymn 'When we walk with the Lord'.
49 N.T. Wright, *The Challenge of Jesus* (SPCK, 2000), p. 61.

50 Crucifixion was used by the Romans as a weapon of terror and subjugation. This public torture spelled out a message of power. The famous Slaves' Revolt led by Spartacus in 73BC led to 6000 of the defeated rebels being crucified along the side of the Appian Way.

51 Jim Elliot's story is told by his widow, Elisabeth Elliot, *Through Gates of Splendor* (Tyndale, 1996).

52 Wright, *The Challenge of Jesus*, p. 146

53 Donald McCullough, *The Trivialization of God* (NavPress, 1995), p. 30.

54 Tom Wright, *Surprised by Hope* (SPCK, 2007), p. 288.

55 For those wishing to grasp a comprehensive view of what the Bible says about the future, Tom Wright's book *Surprised by Hope* provides an excellent summary, especially Chapter 6, 'What the whole world's waiting for'.

56 Bernard of Morlaix wrote this in 1146. It was translated from Latin to English by John M. Neale in 1858.

57 C.S. Lewis, *Christian Reflections* (Eerdmans, 1967), p. 106.

Also by Ian Coffey (with Kim Bush)

Bridges from the Word to the World

Connecting the Bible and everyday living

How can we connect our daily lives with the teaching of the Bible? How can we listen to the news and link what we hear to our faith? How should we as Christians respond to the sights and sounds that surround us every day?

Bridges span—it is what they are made to do. Rivers, valleys, roadways, even stretches of the sea are crossed with ease and journeys that used to take hours are reduced to seconds.

This book is called *Bridges from the Word to the World* because it is designed to span what can feel like a gap between the Bible and the rest of life. It offers short reflections on a wide range of themes and happenings both national and international, linked to relevant Bible passages and short prayers to take into the day.

ORDERFORM

REF	TITLE	PRICE	QTY	TOTAL
385 5	Bridges from the Word to the World	£7.99		
		Postage and packing		
		Donation		
		TOTAL		

POSTAGE AND PACKING CHARGES				
Order value	UK	Europe	Surface	Air Mail
£7.00 & under	£1.25	£3.00	£3.50	£5.50
£7.10–£30.00	£2.25	£5.50	£6.50	£10.00
Over £30.00	FREE	prices on request		

Name ______________________ Account Number __________

Address ______________________________________

______________________ Postcode __________

Telephone Number______________________

Email ______________________________________

Payment by: ❑ Cheque ❑ Mastercard ❑ Visa ❑ Postal Order ❑ Maestro

Card no ☐☐☐☐ ☐☐☐☐ ☐☐☐☐ ☐☐☐☐ ☐☐☐

Valid from ☐☐☐☐ Expires ☐☐☐☐ Issue no. ☐☐☐

Security code* ☐☐☐ *Last 3 digits on the reverse of the card. ESSENTIAL IN ORDER TO PROCESS YOUR ORDER

Shaded boxes for Maestro use only

Signature ______________________ Date __________

All orders must be accompanied by the appropriate payment.

Please send your completed order form to:

BRF, 15 The Chambers, Vineyard, Abingdon OX14 3FE
Tel. 01865 319700 / Fax. 01865 319701 Email: enquiries@brf.org.uk

❑ Please send me further information about BRF publications.

Available from your local Christian bookshop.